Michael Murray

ALBERT SCHWEITZER

Sketches for a Portrait

Jackson Lee Ice

UNIVERSITY
PRESS OF
AMERICA

Lanham • New York • London

THE
ALBERT
SCHWEITZER
INSTITUTE
FOR THE HUMANITIES

University Press of America® Inc.
4720 Boston Way
Lanham, Maryland 20706

3 Henrietta Street
London WC2E 8LU England

Copublished by arrangement with
The Albert Schweitzer Institute for the Humanities

Library of Congress Cataloging-in-Publication Data

Ice, Jackson Lee.
Albert Schweitzer : sketches for a portrait / by Jackson Lee Ice.
p.   cm.
Includes bibliographical references.
1. Schweitzer, Albert, 1875–1965—Contributions in theology.
2. Schweitzer, Albert, 1875–1965—Ethics.   I. Title.
BX4827.S35I2   1994   230'.092—dc20   93–40728 CIP

ISBN 0–8191–9400–X (cloth : alk. paper)

 The paper used in this publication meets the minimum requirements of
American National Standard for Information Sciences—Permanence
of Paper for Printed Library Materials, ANSI Z39.48–1984.

Dedicated to My Children

Heather Ice Bowman, Mark Ice and Shahn Ice

Contents

Foreword

Albert Schweitzer, the person, his work and his ideas became of important interest to Professor Jackson Lee Ice at Harvard University where he wrote his first major piece, *A Critique of Albert Schweitzer's Philosophy of Civilization*. Since that time, he has published numerous articles and books, including *Schweitzer: Prophet of Radical Theology*, which has been called the best work on Schweitzer's Christology.

In August 1991, Jack died leaving a near-complete manuscript of his last book on this great humanitarian, *Albert Schweitzer: Sketches for a Portrait*. His aim was to write a collection of essays investigating questions and issues that have arisen over the years concerning Schweitzer's life and thought. Jack wrote,

> A final assessment of Schweitzer's scholarly contributions as a world figure has not yet been made. Recent misunderstandings and bothersome questions, both real and imaginary, prevent the rendering of a complete portrait. A constant resketching for a more accurate understanding is required, as it is with any complex figure. These studies attempt to do just that. Each essay tries to bring crucial aspects of his thought into sharper focus, each to grapple with some unresolved issue, each to look at Schweitzer from a different angle in order to have a fuller, more accurate understanding of his ideas.

I hope Jack's radically honest attempt to point out misunderstandings, clarify complexities and stress what he considered to be the most interesting aspects of Schweitzer's thought will excite and encourage others to continue Schweitzer's Reverence for Life.

Some of the writing was done in the early 1960s, when Albert Schweitzer was still alive. In these instances, the original tense has been preserved.

The publication of this book would not be possible without the support and encouragement of many. I would like to acknowledge and thank Harold Robles, Founder and President of The Albert Schweitzer Institute for the Humanities (ASIH), and Rhena Schweitzer Miller and Dr. David C. Miller for their continued support and direction in completing this book. I wish additionally to acknowledge the cooperation of Professor Leo Sandon, Chairperson of the Department of Religion at Florida State University.

A special thank you to Michael Murray, organist and member of the

Advisory Board of ASIH, for writing Chapter V, *Schweitzer and Bach*. Thank you also to David Miller for his contribution in organizing and selecting Jack's original notes on Schweitzer and Bach which are included as an appendix. This is intended to afford the reader the opportunity to consider any differences in interpretation or emphasis between Jack's notes and Michael's finished chapter.

Lastly, but not least, I would like to thank the individuals at The Albert Schweitzer Institute who typed, proofread and edited this manuscript, and prepared it for publication: Morgan Avery, Lauren Chisnall, Linus Fung, Maribeth Marsico, James Pouilliard and Susan Preneta. Without their help this book would not have reached its final stage.

M. Marie Ice
Tallahasse, Florida
August 1993

Preface

This volume reflects much of the pilgrimage of Jackson Lee Ice; the decades in which he taught and wrote; and the circle of friends, acquaintances and collaborators who shared his journey. A number of the chapters have been published before as separate articles, but bringing them together in this anthology provides an edge and focus which will be useful to those interested in the legacy of Albert Schweitzer. Jack Ice had an abiding interest in the life, thought and ethics of Schweitzer, and this volume, therefore, is something of a culmination of his work as scholar-teacher.

For all of his interest in ethics, aesthetics, existential phenomenology, theology, and philosophy of religion, Jack Ice was wont to refer to himself as a Schweitzer scholar. Several of these essays move beyond scholarly explication to a frankly apologetic character as Ice engages criticisms of Schweitzer's work which he felt were either analytically inadequate, inaccurate or both. Others attempt to plumb more deeply the implications of the various aspects of Schweitzer's thought. The book as a whole reflects not only Schweitzer's broad range of activity but also Ice's interests and gifts in music and art as well as in the philosophy of religion.

The essays also reflect many of the issues discussed over the past three decades among American theologians, philosophers and ethicists. In Chapter I, first published in *The Hibbert Journal* in 1965, Ice defends criticisms of Schweitzer's alleged paternalism. In Chapter II, a 1976 article in *The Christian Century*, the context is the wake of the death-of-God debate as Ice discusses Schweitzer's "strange mixture of theism and pantheism." In his comparison of radical monotheism (not to be confused with H.R. Niebuhr's development of the concept) and ethical pantheism (Chapter VII) Ice mirrors the concern for ecological ethics as it was discussed in the 1970s. Other pieces in the collection are not so confined to a particular historical context.

The book, finally, reflects the network of associations—loved ones, professional colleagues and friends--who have aided in bringing it to completion. It is as much a tribute to Jackson Lee Ice's person and work as it is an exploration of Albert Schweitzer's life and thought.

Leo Sandon
Tallahassee, Florida
May 1993

Albert Schweitzer by Jackson Lee Ice

CHAPTER ONE

Is Schweitzer a Racist?
1965

The gradual growth of familiarity with the person and work of Albert Schweitzer has now reached a strange climax: so many know him, as it were by reputation and hearsay, and yet so few take the trouble to find out for themselves what he is really like or what he really says and believes. Such familiarity breeds not only contempt, but suspicion among more concerned scholars that such popularization has prematurely rigidified certain misconceptions about him and trapped him between a cult of acclaimers on one hand and a crowd of critics on the other.

The search for glamour without meaning—so characteristic of our age — has seemingly enervated any sober attempt to bring his real significance into focus without exaggeration or bias. As someone has recently written, we have been thinking of Schweitzer for so long as a plaster-sainted missionary that a major engineering operation is required if we are to overthrow irrelevant standards and begin judging him without prejudice. It is true that those caught up in the enthusiasm of the Schweitzer saga tended to idolize the man and gloss over imperfections. Perhaps we are all too greedy to make the thought and life do more than it could do, and be more than it could be.

But it is also true that in the present attempts to stem the tide of hero-worship, the prejudice arising from antagonism and shallow acquaintance must be guarded against. The recent rush of critical "reappraisals" have tended to misrepresent and vitiate what is important. Both idolization and iconoclasm make for poor exchange, both are counterfeit coins; and in the long run such currency must be expunged from the market of fact.

Schweitzer, of course, like every other world figure, has never been free from criticism. But lately the criticisms have become more irrelevant, petty and unfounded. Earlier thinkers such as Oskar Kraus, John Middleton Murray and George Seaver were critically concerned with pertinent points of his ethical and religious thought; now complaints center around his person, his jungle hospital, attitudes and prejudices which he seems to embody, and his failure to be all things to all men.

The most pertinent criticisms now in vogue are those which call our attention to three "fundamental defects" in Schweitzer's outlook and character. They are: his lack of genuine concern for the non-white; his questionable motives for establishing Lambaréné; and his political short-sightedness.

I

Many of the visitors who imposed themselves upon Schweitzer's amenability, "sightseeing" at his "quaint" hospital in Africa, returned home quite disenchanted. They found that not only is the hospital compound shockingly dirty, "more like a menagerie than a hospital," but that Schweitzer is a "fallible, vain, petty, prejudiced" old man[1], a "dictatorial taskmaster" who orders the natives and help around like a bull-necked construction foreman."[2] They speak of these traits with a certain undercurrent of new discovery or disillusionment. Whatever their expectations, they found in Lambaréné, not a saint, but a very human and individualistic person indeed.[3]

In all likelihood these idiosyncratic descriptions are true; he probably is "obstinate and authoritative in a peculiarly Teutonic manner." But though we must take note of them, none of these facts detract from his achievements.

What is really disconcerting is not that these detractors spend time rehearsing Schweitzer's interesting eccentricities, but that they employ such biographical trivia in order to discredit him. For example, how do those who accuse Schweitzer of "possessing only an intellectualized version of the 'white man's burden'" substantiate their claim? Not necessarily by citing cogent facts, but mainly by using an *ad hominem* argument. It reads: "*because* Schweitzer is often dictatorial, prejudiced, pedantic . . . irascible, vain and, on some subjects, obstinately old-fashioned, and *because* he advocates an 'elder brother' attitude toward his primitive laborers, and is a little too sure of himself in his paternal handling of the African," therefore it follows that Schweitzer is merely using Lambaréné for his own ends, and is not sympathetically concerned with the plight of the black man.[4]

Assuming that the statements by themselves are true, the particular conclusions drawn from them do not logically follow. Compliance and neatness are admirable qualities, but are not the only criteria for judgment.

The crucial question here is just what is meant by "only an intellectualized version of the 'white man's burden.'" Does it mean one who only *talks* about helping one's fellow men? Then it does not apply to Schweitzer. Does it mean one who only *play-acts* the part of genuine concern, but brings no real benefit to mankind? Then, again, it cannot apply to this productive life. Does it mean he gives the *impression* that he lacks sympathy in actual contacts with non-whites? Subjective complexes are proverbially difficult to determine, and impressions are often deceptive. Does it mean that Schweitzer's particular *way* of benefiting the destitute African is not as efficacious as any other which might be suggested? Then this is another matter, and must be argued on other grounds.

The question might be stated in another way: "What set of facts or acts could one point to which would *disprove* this indictment against Dr. Schweitzer? What would he have to do, that he has not already done, to prove the integrity of his motives and his genuine sympathy for the people among whom he has lived for so long?" In the face of all he has done, it is difficult to say.

Perhaps we are nearer to an understanding of the indictment, if we express it in the words of one writer:

> He loves the African in the abstract, just as he loves any form of life—a white man, an antelope, a toad, an ant or a palm tree. . . His work could as well have been performed in Brazil or a hundred other places. It is, in fact, an act of personal contrition, a magnificent act, but nothing more, nothing less.[5]

Such criticism might be commendation in disguise; particularly if we realize the strong Kantian strain in Schweitzer's ethical outlook. An act is more moral in direct proportion as it is done out of respect for the moral law, according to Kant, and not for reason of any particular personal benefit or consideration of felicitous consequences. The moral act is its own reward; we are moral not because of any non-moral values which may be realized, but because the moral is reason's universalized postulate autonomously imposed by man upon himself. Such moral duty plays no favorites; we are commanded to love all men (and in Schweitzer's case, *all* life) irrespectively. Schweitzer's life *is* an act of contrition. And I believe it is true his work could as well have been performed in any other place of need. If this is what is meant by Schweitzer's intellectualized version of the "white man's burden," then it is a defect one could easily wish more people possessed.

Even if Schweitzer's attitudes and actions seem too calculated and bound by the philosopher's rational version of moral duty, and even if his missionary approach to the problem of human misery can be called into question as pathetically antiquated, it would not necessarily disprove his sincerity or his genuine affection for the peoples to whom he has given so much. And certainly no recitation of personal defects can serve as a basis for such a serious charge, particularly in the face of so much evidence to the contrary.

II

Another criticism made of Schweitzer is that he used Lambaréné to further his own ends, mainly to bring attention to his writings on ethics. "Lambaréné is more important to Schweitzer than he to it," it is claimed.

It is well known that when Schweitzer resolved to become a jungle doctor in 1904, he was severely criticized by relatives and friends for jeopardizing a promising career. If intellectual fame had been his main motivation, Schweitzer could have remained in Europe, for instance, as the principal of the Strasbourg Theological School, or as a professor of New Testament studies, or as a professor of philosophy at some other university of renown. If he had done so, he would have had time to write many more books and attain greater prominence as a philosopher than he now has.

As it was, he needed neither Lambaréné nor his later writings on ethical philosophy to be recognized as a scholar. His works on Kant, Jesus, Paul, Nietzsche and Bach, written prior to his African sojourn, were independently acclaimed as epoch-making books. As to his later writings, I am convinced that they too would have been known and esteemed whether he had become a missionary or not.

However, that his ethic was enlivened by his own example of reverence for life, does not preclude its appeal or its profundity. Or, to put it in another way, that his activities were enlightened by his later writings on reverence for life, does not preclude their significance nor cast doubt on his integrity as a humanitarian.

It ought to be remembered that Schweitzer made his momentous decision *before* he decided to write his philosophy of culture. He also gave up his own organ playing and his scholastic activities when he left for Africa. The opportunity to write again came about unexpectedly when he was taken prisoner during the First World War and confined at the prison camps of Garaison and St. Remy.

If Schweitzer sought only to call attention to his moral philosophy (then as yet unwritten) by relinquishing a promising career in Europe, struggling through six years of intense medical training, and sacrificing family, friends and health to live amongst the natives in French Equatorial Africa, most would agree it was surely a very costly, indeed ludicrous, way to advertise.

However, perhaps what is meant by this particular indictment is that by now, after fifty years, the hospital at Lambaréné has become for Schweitzer a symbol of all that he has tried to do and say, a harbinger of the moral possibilities of the human spirit which has spelled hope for so many years. His life's work has gone into it; it is a place dowered with personal memories, as personal as his autograph and as incapable of change. And because of this, some charge, it stands in changeless isolation, an anachronism in modern-day Africa.

If this is what is implied, I think we must agree, for I believe it is one of the reasons why Schweitzer stubbornly refuses to go modern. This and the fact he sees no urgent reason why his way of operating the hospital should change.[6] But this is not a serious charge. Those who make it do not realize perhaps that Lambaréné is not just a mission hospital; it is now, not only to Schweitzer, but to a great many people, a symbol also. They forget a much greater value can be realized if it is so and remains so.

That Lambaréné is more important to Schweitzer than he to it, *in this sense* is not an argument for its ineffectiveness or his guile. It is made because we would like to see it serve more effectively. But perhaps we ought to be thankful that it exists at all.

III

The most serious indictment made against Schweitzer is that he does not understand the need of the non-whites in their present struggle for independence. It is claimed he does not sympathize with their growing spirit of nationalism. He is still living under the illusion that "the great white father knows best," they say, and thus he views the whole problem in a paternalistic manner which smacks of European colonialism.

These accusations stem partially from several remarks Schweitzer made in his 1954 Nobel Address in which he spoke of the growth of a "virulent variety" of nationalism among the smaller nations of the world, and its endangering "a long history of peace."

Schweitzer has always been suspicious of nationalism as a solution to any human problem. As history has witnessed, it too easily degenerates into fanatical patriotism and becomes a cloak behind which hide racial prejudice, economic aggression and ignoble paternalism. Such a course among the nations of Western culture has been one of the main factors of its decline.[7] At present he regards it as "the greatest obstacle to international understanding" among the leading nations. Hence his fear lest the newer states will make it their sole aim, and incur needless unrest and bloodshed for themselves and others.

Schweitzer's views on nationalism must not be taken as an argument favoring colonialism or the continued subjugation of the smaller nations. If one reads the entire speech, and his many remarks elsewhere, it is obvious he is not inferring that the colonial nations have enjoyed a utopian peace whilst under European domination, nor that they must remain silent. In fact, he states the opposite.

His solution to the problem of world peace moves on another level. He is addressing mainly the larger nations, those in control; he is challenging them to be humane enough to aid the underprivileged peoples to grow and become independent, without ignominiously forcing them to choose between disrespectful domination and fanatical nationalism, between exploitation, under the guise of "aiding them until they are ready," and abandonment. He is placing a greater obligation on their shoulders than merely to step aside and allow self-rule. In an earlier writing Schweitzer set forth a bill of rights for the African in which, after speaking of their "fundamental right" to habitation, soil, labor, justice and education, he states that "the only way to defend and extend the other rights already enumerated is to develop a new stable social organization."[8] Our goal then must be the eventual formation of an orderly, productive and efficient self-rule of these peoples. But at present, particularly in certain regions of Africa, allowing them freedom by a complete withdrawal, without the proper guidance and adequate aid, would be the same, in many respects, as abandonment. The first step in aiding any primitive people toward intelligent self-rule is providing morally-concerned and enlightened leadership. This we have not given them, and we are suffering the consequences.

Schweitzer may be naive in believing that nationalism is not an essential element in the emancipation of the world's long-dominated peoples, or in not recognizing fully enough the danger of our "civilizing mission" withholding independence too long. If this is so, then let us point it out. But it is erroneous to believe he is in favor of maintaining the colonial status of these emerging nations, in the sense in which we are accustomed to using this phrase.

Usually, to support the above accusation, Schweitzer's paternalistic treatment of the natives is mentioned: his "elder brother" attitude and his feeling that "the black man is still a child."

I admit some of his words on this point are puzzling. But I wonder if many have not made an unjustifiable leap, from his handling of the workers and patients in his own particular situation, to his views on the matter on an international scale? To equate the type of leadership which he exhibits at Lambaréné with that of advocating white supremacy is not only erroneous, but damaging to a much needed spirit which moves in the opposite direction. Having to live among mainly primitive people, still lulled to sleep by the rhythms of the primeval forest and made incorrigible at times by their child-like irresponsibility and fearful superstitions, is a little different from formulating general political programs for the modern educated black. His personal paternal attitude at his hospital, the result, it seems, of expediency rather than prejudice, must not be translated into a stand for racism. If Schweitzer possesses an "elder brother" attitude toward the natives, it is in the spirit "I am my brother's elder *brother*," and not "I am my brother's *keeper*," so often exhibited by the condescending air of the so-called Christian nations.

Dr. W. E. DuBois, emeritus professor of sociology, Atlanta University, though critical of Schweitzer because "he had no grasp of what modern exploitation means, of what imperial colonialism has done to the world," could conclude "that this man was [the black's] friend and benefactor there was no question. If more of his people were like him, not only Africa but Asia, not only far-off lands but near-by slums, might be raised to decency, efficiency, and real civilization."[9]

It is a specious defense of our shortcomings to condemn such a man as Schweitzer for not extricating us from the evils which we ourselves by neglect have brought about, or for not being a paragon of perfection, at a time when we could use his influence in the world to political advantage. Merely because Schweitzer has remained strangely silent on some issues of international importance, or because he apparently has no knowledge of the new generation of Africans, or of the intellectual and emotional tides sweeping the continent, I find it difficult to condemn him. To chide a man who has done so much, for not doing more, is unjust.

We must stop looking at the old-fashioned sun helmet that Schweitzer wears—viewing it hypersensitively as symbolic of an outmoded political philosophy—and turn our attention to understanding the ideas and spirit of the man beneath it. Evidence points to the fact that his whole mission in life was a personal protest against the very evils for which his unjustified critics now accuse him. The evils of racial prejudice and European domination, which bind the peoples of the underdeveloped countries even more firmly in the chains of hate and oppression, have been the very targets of his words and deeds.

IV

In conclusion, I would add that it is doubly difficult to understand any great personality where ordinary labels do not seem to apply. The mark of genius is always complexity; and no person escapes contradictions. What adds to the difficulty of understanding him is not only his social marginality, but the fact that Schweitzer took his stand in an intensity of awareness which is isolated from ordinary solutions and common aims of twentieth century man. In this sense he is unique; hence he will continue to be the subject of scorn and amazement.

However, if Schweitzer's actions and words are at times puzzling and disappointing, or have a distasteful, European, paternalistic cast about them, I suggest they be reappraised in the light of the fuller context of his life and thought. The larger perspective, I believe, if it will not solve, will at least placate some of the doubts about his genuine concern for the African black, his motivations in Lambaréné, and his apparent political shortsightedness.

As Norman Cousins wrote:

Albert Schweitzer will not be immune from attack. There may be a period of carping and intended exposure, most of it with an air of fresh discovery and all of it in a mood of disillusion. But in the long run the inconsistencies and paradoxes will be as nothing alongside the real meaning of Albert Schweitzer and his place in history. Few men of our century have come closer to attaining the Greek idea of the whole man—the thinker, the leader, the man of action, the scientist, the artist. But like all great figures in history, he becomes real not despite his frailties but because of them.[10]

Notes

[1]Smith Hempstone, *Miami Herald*, 23 Dec. 1962.

[2]Peter Grose, *The Florida Times-Union*, 18 Nov. 1962.

[3]See: John Gunther, "Inside Africa;" Negley Farson, "A Mirror for Narcissus;" Gerald McKnight, "Verdict on Schweitzer;" The British reporters: James Cameron (*News Chronicle*), John Russell (*Sunday Times*).

[4]C. W. M. Gell, "Dr. Schweitzer—A Reassessment," *The Hibbert Journal*, July 1957, p. 330 ff.

[5]Smith Hempstone, *Miami Herald*, 23 Dec. 1962.

[6]"Despite such squalor, Schweitzer's institution has a good medical record, and the city's Europeans generally choose it over the new government hospital. Few hospitals anywhere can offer such a dedicated staff . . ." (*Time* magazine, 21 June 1963).

[7]Schweitzer, *Philosophy of Civilization*, p. 29 ff.

[8]Schweitzer, "The Relations of the White to the Coloured Races," *Contemporary Review*, Jan. 1928.

[9]W.E. DuBois, "The Black Man and Albert Schweitzer," *The Albert Schweitzer Jubilee Book*, A. A. Roback (ed.), p. 125.

[10]Norman Cousins, *Dr. Schweitzer of Lambaréné* (Harper & Brothers, New York, 1960), p. 219.

CHAPTER TWO

Did Schweitzer Believe in God?
1976

During the Schweitzer Centennial Symposium at UNESCO in Paris, psychoanalyst Erich Fromm raised a pertinent question: "Is Schweitzer's religious ethic of Reverence for Life dependent upon a belief in God?" The question is not as easy as it appears, but it is my contention that *mutatis mutandis*, the ethic of Reverence for Life is not dependent upon a belief in God.

A 1967 journal article by Erwin R. Jacobi discusses a previously unpublished letter from Schweitzer dated three years before his death, in which Schweitzer makes the following statement:

> Hence there arises the question whether the religious ethic of Love is possible without the belief in an ethical God and World Sovereign, or knowledge of this God, which can be replaced by a belief in Him. Here I dare say that the ethical religion of love can exist without the belief in a world-ruling divine personality which corresponds to such an ethical religion.[1]

I

According to Schweitzer's own words, then, the ethic of Reverence for Life is *not* founded upon a belief in a personal God. This conclusion may seem strange to those who regard Schweitzer as one of the twentieth century's greatest religious figures. It is disconcerting enough to realize how theologically unorthodox—indeed, revolutionary—he was. But it may be even more unnerving for some to find that the concept of a Supreme Being apparently does not play a central role in his religious philosophy, at least not in his ethical teachings.

But the answer, as well as the question, contains implications requiring further clarification. First, note the particular terms Schweitzer used: he said that the religion of love is not dependent upon belief in a "divine personality" (*Gottespersonlichkeit*) or "World Sovereign" (*Weltherrscher*). The more essential and intriguing question is whether Schweitzer believed in God at all! This must be answered first; for the answer illuminates the secondary issue of the apparent non-theistic basis of his ethic.

For the general reader, the primary question usually comes later, if at all —partly because of Schweitzer's "halo image" and his prepossessing style of writing. His ideas are so unpretentiously expressed in familiar language interwoven with biblical phraseology, God-talk and personal spiritual insights that the agnostic, radical outcroppings of his religious viewpoint are ignored. Most readers assume Schweitzer's belief in God without debate. But with more critical examination of the deeper structures of his thought, the issue inevitably arises and demands analysis.

Though the question "Did Schweitzer believe in God?" is legitimate, it usually anticipates a Yes-or-No answer which is difficult to give. An attempt to point to the multi-functional meanings of the term "God" is often taken as a dodge. But to ask, "Do you believe in God?" expecting a simple categorical Yes or No is naive. To continue to draw up—as many of our denominational leaders do — battle lines with humanists on one side and theists on the other is specious and still reflects the popular, but otiose, approach to the whole debate. One of the invaluable consequences of the contemporary theological furor, particularly the death-of-God debate, has been the resolve to root out this jejune approach to the God-problem and to search for alternative categories of reflection which match the complexity of the problem.

II

Still the question must be asked. In regard to Schweitzer, the reply has to be Yes or No. If by God is meant the Father Almighty, maker of heaven and earth, who redeems his children by the atonement and sacrifice of his Son Jesus Christ according to the predestined plan of salvation revealed in the Bible and ascribed to by the Christian churches, then the answer obviously is No — Schweitzer does not believe in God.

If by God is meant *a* Being, supremely conscious, all-knowing, all-powerful, completely self-sufficient, who determines all things by divine moral purpose, the answer is again No. If by God is meant the Ground of Being, the Essence of Being, the Absolute, the *Weltgeist*, and all similar expressions, the reply is still No, for according to Schweitzer such terms "denote nothing actual, but something conceived in abstractions which for that reason is also absolutely meaningless."[2]

If by God is meant a conceptual construct used within a certain linguistic frame of reference for the purpose of arousing religious emotions and ethical sentiments in solemn assemblies, the answer must again be No. Schweitzer gives little indication that he believes that analyzing the function of a term linguistically or sociologically solves the problem of the reality or unreality of God.

What then does he mean by God? Schweitzer's disenchantment with theological conceptions of God and his passionate belief in the reality of human spirituality involved him in a quest that inevitably forced his intellectual and moral concerns to move beyond traditional theism. "It is my fate and my destiny . . . to ponder on the question of how much ethics and religion can be comprised in a *Weltanschauung* which dares to be inconclusive."[3]

What does he mean by "inconclusive"? He means that he is forced to ponder to what extent humanity can continue to be religious in a universe devoid of pre-established meaning, moral purpose and certainty; he means a religious outlook that must continue to function within the impossibility of using God any longer as a religious a priori, filler of our intellectual gaps, or solver of all problems; he means a world view that must remain painfully honest and open-ended yet at the same time will be optimistic, ethical and life-affirming.

Schweitzer had his own variation on the death-of-God theme. It comes in the form of an ethical mysticism or "ethical pantheism" which he described as the "inevitable synthesis of theism and pantheism." No mention is made of a Supreme Being in his own religious philosophy, only of a mysterious life-force or universal will-to-live which appears as a creative-destructive force in the world around us and as a will-to-self-realization-and-love within us. Everything is in the grasp of this life-force, this "infinite, inexplicable, forward-urging will in which all Being is grounded."[4]

For several reasons he does not speak of "God" when referring to the "Universal Will": first, because he arrives at knowledge of the will-to-live through reason and not by revelation or faith; second, because the life-force is not a thing or a person; and finally, because the usual connotations associated with the term "God" misrepresent what he is trying to say. "It has always been my practice," said Schweitzer, "not to say anything when speaking as a philosopher that goes beyond the absolutely logical exercise of thought. That is why I never speak of 'God' in philosophy, but only of 'universal will-to-live' which meets me in a two-fold way: as creative will outside me, and ethical will within me."[5]

If Schweitzer speaks of God at all, he does so in human, spiritual terms rather than theological, metaphysical terms. In his typical humanistic, ethico-mystical way of thinking, he points to a belief in the "evolution of human spirituality" where "the higher this development in the individual is, the greater his awareness of God."[6]

III

Now the answer to the original question raised by Erich Fromm can be modified for accuracy's sake. Because of the multiple meanings which accrue to the protosymbol "God" and because of Schweitzer's own particular reference to the term, it can be answered both in the affirmative and the negative. That is not equivocation. If one accepts the word "God" with its usual conventional connotations and traditional meanings, then the answer is No, as Schweitzer himself made clear. He found that the facts do not support such an anthropomorphic or optimistic postulate. On the other hand, if one understands his concept of ethical pantheism—which holds that the ethico-rational, or spiritual, proclivities of humanity are potentially grounded in, and part of, a universal telos or will—then the answer is Yes: his ethical philosophy of Reverence for Life is dependent, in theory as well as in practice, upon a belief in God.

The phrase "reverence for life" is holophrastic; it means and represents many things for Schweitzer. It does not serve merely as an admonition or moral maxim as to what one ought to do. It represents more than just his ethic; it includes his world view; it is the heart of his religious philosophy. This is why he could say, "And this ethic, profound, universal, has the significance of a religion. It *is* religion."[7] Giving ontological status to the term "life" or "will-to-live," the phrase "reverence for life" becomes a capsulized expression of Schweitzer's "mysticism of reality" or "ethical pantheism." It signifies a reverence or veneration for the Universal Will or Reality in which all life and all things are grounded. Through this attitude, according to Schweitzer, humanity seeks to be united with the Cosmic Will, and thus strives to overcome the estrangement (*Selbstentzweiung*) which mysteriously and painfully exists between the blind, groping, truculent forms of energy in the world at large and the purposive, unorally concerned form, or will-to-love, which humanity discovers in itself.

IV

This is Schweitzer's concept of God. It may be a puzzling one—this strange mixture of theism and pantheism—but it functions as a God-concept for him and formed the basis of his thought. For many it will fall short of a true theistic belief, and appear too meager to serve as a firm foundation for a religious philosophy of life.

Perhaps the reader can now appreciate the complexities involved in arriving at a univocal answer where Schweitzer's belief in God is concerned —and for that matter, the belief of any innovative thinker in the field who has moved far beyond the strictures of traditional theism which still blind us to alternative modes of insight and expression.

Most people, I find, demand a finished edifice of faith before they enter with confidence to pray. Certainly the universe has more to offer by way of guaranteeing their traditional beliefs than what Schweitzer proffers, they contend. But according to Schweitzer, if we are honest—and our situation demands nothing less—it does not. He openly admits that his religious philosophy is incomplete, but he insists that it is enough.

> The surmisings and the longings of all deep religiousness are contained in the ethics of Reverence for Life. This religiousness, however, does not build up for itself a complete philosophy, but resigns itself to leave the cathedral by necessity unfinished. It is only able to finish the choir. Yet in this, true piety celebrates a living and continuous divine service.[8]

In an age such as ours in which the old theistic idols have died or have been broken, it must be more than important that such pioneers as Schweitzer have had the insight and courage to accept the challenge to take the next steps toward the light and show us, in deed as well as in thought, how to "sing the Lord's song in a strange land."

Notes

[1]Erwin R. Jacobi, "Fromm Sein. Gedanken zu einem Brief von Albert Schweitzer." *Divine Light*, Vol. 2, No. 1, June 1967. *"Also ist die Frage vorhanden, ob die ethische Frommigkeit der Liebe moglich ist, ohne den Glauben an den ethischen Gott und Weltherrscher oder die Erkenntnis dieses Gottes, die durch einen Glauben an ihn zu eretzen ist. Da wage ich zu sagen, dass die ethische Religion der Liebe bestehen kann ohne den Glauben an eine ihr entsprechende, die Welt leitende Gottespersonlichkeit."*

[2]Albert Schweitzer, *The Philosophy of Civilization*, trans. C. T. Campion (The Macmillan Company, 1949), p. 304.

[3]Oskar Kraus, *Albert Schweitzer* (London: Adams and Charles Black, Ltd., 1944), p. 43.

[4]Albert Schweitzer, *Kultur und Ethik* (Munich: Biederstein Verlag, 1948), p. 211.

[5]Kraus, *Albert Schweitzer*, p. 42.

[6]Norman Cousins, *Dr. Schweitzer of Lambaréné* (Harper and Brothers, 1960), pp. 190-191.

[7]George Seaver, *Albert Schweitzer: The Man and His Mind* (Harper and Brothers, 1947), p. 342.

[8]Schweitzer, *Kultur und Ethik*, pp. 243-244.

CHAPTER THREE

Was Schweitzer a Mystic After All?
1978

What are we to make of a thinker who sets forth a philosophy of "ethical mysticism," and yet maintains that "all real progress in the world is in the last analysis produced by rational thought"? How are we to understand one who says: "Every world- and life-view which is to satisfy thought is mysticism," and yet states that "mysticism which exists for itself alone is the salt which has lost its savor"? What do we do with a writer who believes that "all profound philosophy, all deep religion, are ultimately a struggle for ethical mysticism," and yet asserts that, "mysticism is not a friend of ethics, but a foe"? And what does he mean when he claims that "reflection, when pursued to the end, leads . . . to a living mysticism, which is . . . a necessary element of thought"?[1]

These curious claims by Albert Schweitzer lead one to wonder what he means by mysticism and whether, in the face of being variously labeled "idealist," "rationalist," "existentialist," and "radical" free-thinker, he is a mystic after all. Has he for some eccentric reason stretched the term beyond recognition? Or has he brought new illumination to a complex and frequently misunderstood subject?

I

Schweitzer writes that the main goal of religion is "to attain spiritual unity with infinite Being." "We are not satisfied to belong to the universe only as physical beings," he stated in The Gifford Lectures delivered at Edinburgh University in November 1934, but want "to belong to it also as spiritual critics"; we aim "at our spirit becoming one with the spirit universe." For "only in spiritual unity can we give meaning to our lives and find strength to suffer and to act."[2] This raises a crucial question: "How can I conceive of myself as being in the world and at the same time in God?"— implying, of course, the further question: How can one attain such a unity?[3]

In traditional religious belief it is by some form of mysticism that humanity can achieve such a goal. Schweitzer apparently concurs; but what kind of mysticism does he propose?

Schweitzer notes two basic kinds of mysticism: "primitive" and "developed."[4] The "primitive" concept of union with the divine is naive and usually confined to super-earthly forces placated to assure personal and group protection, power, healing and immortal life. It seeks participation in these suprasensuous powers by means of secret rites which include ecstatic dances, incantations, auto-hypnosis, mortification of the flesh and drug-induced trances. This type he also called "magical mysticism." Its reoccurrence throughout history and its reappearance in our time demonstrate its latent virility and chthonic appeal.

The "developed" form arises "whenever thought makes the ultimate effort to concentrate on the relation of personality to the universal." Moreover:

> When the conception of the universal is reached and a man reflects upon his relation to the totality of being and to Being in itself, the resultant mysticism becomes widened, deepened and purified. The entrance into the super-earthly and eternal then takes place through an act of thinking. In this act the conscious personality raises itself above that illusion of the senses which makes him regard himself as in bondage . . . to the earthly and temporal. [5]

This type Schweitzer calls "intellectual mysticism," to be found among "the Brahmans, in Buddha, Platonism, Stoicism, in Spinoza, Schopenhauer and Hegel."

Though there are many varieties of "intellectual mysticism" that have appeared "according to time and place," Schweitzer emphasizes two forms which are radically distinguished from each other: "abstract mysticism" and "ethical mysticism." The distinctions between the two are, in his opinion, crucial. The former (characterized also by the terms "God-mysticism," "passive" or "supraethical" mysticism) ends in world denial, affirms that Ultimate Reality is knowable, and asserts that one can, by means of special mental and spiritual powers, attain union with the Infinite. Ethical mysticism, on the other hand (also called "mysticism of actuality"), results in world- and life-affirmation, holds that the World-Spirit or God remains ultimately a mystery, and bases its incomplete view of the nature of things on an encompassing life view. This is the mysticism which he identifies with his philosophy of Reverence for Life.

II

Mysticism has generally been associated—and still is, unfortunately—with the more dramatic types of transcendental, ascetic mysticism of the

Eastern religions. Failure to recognize the appearance of other forms makes the task of understanding mysticism in general, and Schweitzer's thought in particular, doubly difficult. If one has in mind only what Schweitzer designates as "abstract" mysticism, then he cannot be regarded as a mystic and may be accused of misusing the term. His mysticism is certainly not of the conventional kind, and his usage of the term entails none of the traditional characteristics. It does not involve any of the esoteric, theosophical, or *via negativa* ways of knowing. It is not a matter of visions, ecstasies, revelations or occult experiences. There is no separate transcendental realm of Being with which we try to make contact; neither does Schweitzer believe in the identification of the self with the Infinite, nor regard the Absolute as the all-absorbing Reality and the self and world as illusory.

Specific criticisms of traditional mysticism offered by Schweitzer are most informative. "Abstract mysticism," he claims, is first of all purely an intellectual act, a symbolic relationship in which subjectivity converses with itself. Such heightened acts of contemplation lure the mind from the actual to the imaginative. "It becomes a pure act of consciousness, and leads to a spirituality which is just as bare of content as the hypothetical absolute."[6]

Second, instead of being a means, such mysticism mistakenly becomes its own ultimate goal. "The great danger for all mysticism is that of . . . making the spirituality associated with the being-in-eternity an end in itself . . . It does not urge [one] born again to new life, to live as a new person . . . in the world."[7] Third, if it remains consistent with its view of reality as transcendent and with its ideal goal of spiritual absorption, it inevitably results in a withdrawal from active participation in worldly affairs:

> All attempts to extract living religion from pure monistic God-mysticism are foredoomed to failure . . . God-mysticism remains a dead thing. The becoming-one of the finite will with the Infinite acquires a content only when it is experienced both as quiescence . . . and at the same time as a "being-taken-possession-of" by the will of love, which . . . strives in us to become act."[8]

Only by an outlook on life and the world which is active and affirmative can human beings hope to succeed in fulfilling themselves as well as their religious ideals.

Because this is true, "abstract mysticism" attains, in the fourth place, only to an ethic of passive self-perfection devoid of ethics. Hence, it is not ethical in the full sense at all; it is "supraethical":

> How difficult it is for the intellectual mysticism of the being-in-God to reach an ethic is seen in Spinoza. Even in Christian mysticism . . . it is often the semblance of ethics rather than ethics itself which is preserved. There

is always the danger that the mystic will experience the eternal as absolute passivity, and will consequently cease to regard ethical existence as the highest manifestation of spirituality.[9]

Finally, "abstract mysticism" claims too much; it is self-deceptive in asserting that it offers a way to attain to knowledge of Infinite Being. Despite its insistence on special transcendental ways of knowing, Schweitzer finds its claims too ambitious. Traditional mysticism freely recognizes the limitations of all worldly knowledge, yet does not with the same honesty admit the tentativeness of its own intuitive assertions. We are forced to face the sobering fact that in any ultimate sense "the World-Spirit and world events remain to us incomprehensible."[10] Indeed, our knowledge of the Universe as well as our role within it lead deeper and deeper into the impenetrable mystery of Being. To become united with the so-called World-Spirit in thought or spiritual absorption, however pure or transcendent, is impossible, for in reality we remain in ignorance of it.

In the face of these indictments, what kind of mysticism is it that Schweitzer believes can, and must, remain a requisite feature of a rational world view?

III

We must, first of all, regard mystical experience and insight as a means, not as an end. Mysticism is a useful servant but a poor master. It must stand at the service of rational thought as a necessary or completing element in the search for an optimistic and ethical world view. "Mysticism," says Schweitzer "must never be thought to exist for its own sake. It is not a flower, but only the calyx of a flower. Ethics is the flower."[11]

Epistemologically speaking, Schweitzer's view of mysticism is in part synonymous with "creative insight," "intellectual vision" or "intuitive perception." He does not regard such experiences as contrary to reason. Even though Schweitzer, emphasizing the impenetrable mystery of existence which surrounds us, says that all deep thought which thinks itself out to a conclusion wades into the waters of the "nonrational," or of the mystical —he does not mean by this the irrational. His cognitive mysticism is similar to Tillich's "ecstatic reason." While Tillich speaks of "controlling reason," "receiving reason," and "ecstatic reason" (as a form of the latter), Schweitzer speaks of "intellect", "elemental reason", and "mystic insight" (also a form of the latter). There is a striking similarity here, even to the agreement that ecstatic reason "completes" and does not necessarily contradict thought. Such an intuitive or ecstatic insight often possesses a compelling urgency that lends it the character of logical necessity; i.e., at times the vision seems to impress itself upon cognitive awareness with forceful cogency. This is what Schweitzer means, I am sure, by mystical insights being a necessary element of deep thought.

Second, according to Schweitzer we must shift the focus of mysticism from the transcendent to the immanent, from the mystery of the abstract to the mystery of the concrete. It is not the infinite which is truly mysterious, but the finite. "We must . . . . abandon abstract mysticism, and turn to the mysticism which is alive."[12] Instead of becoming devoted to an abstract principle of Being or the Transcendent, we become devoted to the various concrete manifestations of Being as such and release our energies upon them. "It is only through the manifestations of Being, and only through those with which I enter into relations, that my being has any intercourse with infinite Being."[13]

Schweitzer's ethical mysticism begins with a reflective observation of the finite world ("I am urge-to-life"), moves to an empirical generalization ("in the midst of other wills-to-live"), is made cosmic by an intuitive insight, which is the completing or mystical element of thought ("*all* is part of a cosmic or universal will-to-live"), and returns to the finite for experiential verification in ethical participation ("Ethics alone can put me in true relationship with the universe by my serving it, cooperating with it; not by trying to understand it . . . . It is through community of life, not community of thought, that I abide in harmony . . . ").[14] Hence it is a mysticism not of the eternal but the transient, not of the infinite but the finite. It is a nature mysticism or ethical vitalism imbued with spirituality. What he wrote of St. Paul can be said of himself: "In him mysticism is combined with a non-mystical conception of the world."[15]

And last, the spiritual unity with Being which the mystic desires is for Schweitzer attained through giving expression to the natural proclivity within us of the will-to-relatedness, or love, and by becoming united in ethical concern with all forms of life in the world about us.

Schweitzer was firmly convinced that one of the shortcomings of all world religions is that they regard ethics as ultimately separated from spirituality, as is the general rule in Eastern religions, or as myopically identified with the total meaning of religion, as is the case generally in the West. In both instances, religion suffers a loss: either spirituality or ethics goes begging, or one or the other is regarded as a mere appendage. To remedy this, Schweitzer's own position asserts that the spiritual and ethical dimensions can be, and indeed are, inexorably bound together. He finds both naturally and logically united in his religious ethic of Reverence for Life. How is this so?

If I am inwardly made aware of the immediate and obvious fact that "I am will-to-live [which includes the will-to-love] amidst other wills-to-live" and I *act* upon this, my *theoretical* knowledge passes over into *experiential* knowledge. I feel a kinship with all existence (*all* is will-to-live), not abstractly, but existentially. If I then strive out of this instinctive reverence for life to be united with all Life, I fulfill at the same time both my will-to-human-relatedness and will-to-cosmic-relatedness; I am then rooted ethically as well as spiritually. "Our thought," says Schweitzer, "seeks ever to attain harmony with the mysterious Spirit of the Universe. To be complete, such harmony must be both active and passive. That is to say, we seek harmony both in deed and in thought."[16]

The uniting of oneself in ethical action to other life, when all life is seen under the aegis of the Cosmic or Universal Will-to-Live, is what Schweitzer calls "ethical mysticism."

> To relate oneself in the spirit of reverence for life to the multiform manifestations of the will-to-live which together constitute the world is ethical mysticism ... the essence of which is just this: that out of my unsophisticated and naive existence in the world there comes, as a result of thought about self and the world, spiritual self-devotion to the mysterious infinite Will which is continuously manifested in the universe.[17]

In this ethical becoming-one with all life, Schweitzer realizes the spiritual becoming-one with the Primal Source of Being to which all life belongs.

Hence the ethical and the spiritual are founded in the same reality, never to become separated again. We seek union with the same reality upon which the basic principle of the moral is grounded: the Life-Force which includes the will-to-relatedness or love. The proclivity toward devotion to others, expressed naturally in us as pity, sympathy and concern, is part of the same urge toward cosmic rootedness or union that we feel. "There is therefore," said Schweitzer, "dominant in it [Reverence for Life] a spirituality which carries in itself in elemental form the impulse to action. The gruesome truth that spirituality and ethics are two different things no longer holds good. Here the two are one and the same."[18]

We also realize, as a result of Schweitzer's type of mysticism, that world- and life-negation or pessimism is now incongruous, and a purely passive spirituality or religious quiescence becomes impossible.

This then is what Schweitzer means by "ethical mysticism." It means that his ethical theory, and hence his religious philosophy in turn, has, by means of an encompassing or mystical insight, ontological significance as well as moral urgency and rational cogency.

Notes

[1]Albert Schweitzer, *The Philosophy of Civilization*, trans. C. T. Campion (The Macmillan Co., 1949), pp. 54, 56, 301, 303.

[2]Albert Schweitzer, *Indian Thought and Its Development*, trans. Mrs. Charles Russell (Boston: Beacon Press, 1952), p. viii.

[3]Albert Schweitzer, *Christianity and the Religions of the World*, trans. J. Powers (New York: Doubleday, Doran., 2nd ed., 1939), p. 26.

[4]Albert Schweitzer, *The Mysticism of Paul the Apostle*, trans. W. Montgomery and F. C. Burkitt (London: A. & C. Black, 1931), p. 1.

[5]*Ibid.*, p. 1-2.

[6]*Civilization*, p. 302.

[7]*Mysticism*, p. 297.

[8]*Ibid.*, p. 378-79.

[9]*Ibid.*, p. 297.

[10]*Indian Thought*, p. 263.

[11]*Civilization,* p. 304.

[12]*Ibid.*, p. 304.

[13]*Ibid.*, p. 305.

[14]Albert Schweitzer, "The Ethics of Reverence for Life," *Christendom*, Vol. 1, No. 2 (Winter 1936), p. 233-34.

[15]*Mysticism*, p. 4.

[16]"Ethics," p. 234.

[17]*Civilization*, p. 79.

[18]*Ibid.*, p. 305.

CHAPTER FOUR

What Albert Schweitzer Believed about Jesus
1985

The final assessment of Albert Schweitzer's *The Quest of the Historical Jesus* and its full impact on biblical theology has not yet been made. The furor stirred by the book's 1905 appearance soon abated, and the controversial stream of ideas it released seemingly evaporated in the sands of rejection and neglect. But one only has to scan the New Testament literature produced during the past 15 years to realize that the underground spring it opened up has now resurfaced with surprising vitality. From Jurgen Moltmann's claim that Schweitzer's rediscovery of eschatology for our age is "undoubtedly one of the most important events in recent Protestant theology"[1] to Lou Silberman's more recent agreement with Schweitzer that the abiding in Jesus cannot be disengaged from the apocalyptic, historical forms in which it worked itself out, it is obvious that a serious re-appreciation of Schweitzer's contributions to New Testament scholarship is taking place.

The revival is bringing with it a recognition of prior misreadings that even today remain obstacles to an accurate appraisal of Schweitzer's ideas. For example, most assume that Schweitzer was presenting in detail his own hypotheses concerning Jesus in *The Quest of the Historical Jesus,* when in fact, as the original title, *Geschichte der Lebens-Jesu-Forschund* (A History of the Lives-of-Jesus Research), should have signaled, he was mainly engaged in writing a comprehensive study of previous New Testament research (it covers no less than 67 authors!).

Schweitzer did set forth a fuller statement of his own conclusions in an earlier work translated under the English title *The Mystery of the Kingdom of God.* Those who wish to know the more detailed presentation of his own position must read this—something not all critics have done. Also, the *Quest* we have in English is only the first edition. Many are unaware that Schweitzer extensively reworked and enlarged by 241 pages a second edition, published in 1913 just prior to his leaving for Africa, which has never been fully translated into English.

But important as the reconsideration of Schweitzer's insights is for Christian thought, the new debate has shed little light on one of the most curious things about him: the personal role Jesus played in his life. Schweitzer's attachment to Jesus, which is at times characterized by an almost childlike simplicity, seems incongrous with his scholarly views. He speaks of Jesus as the "master of our lives," the "Lord of our ethical wills" and "the one truly great man," and yet he finds him "a child of his age" whose late-Jewish apocalyptic vision of the Kingdom makes him "a stranger to our times"; who was in error about the consummation of history; and who suffered and died in disappointment. He realizes that a critical-historical study of the Bible does not support the Church's doctrine of the Virgin Birth, the divinity of Christ, the Atonement, the miracles, or the inerrancy of Scripture, and yet he can say, "Not for a single moment have I had to struggle for my conviction that in him is the supreme spiritual and religious authority"[2] "Jesus has simply taken me prisoner since my childhood . . . My going to Africa was an act of obedience to Jesus."[3] In a moving passage in the *Quest*, Schweitzer describes the drama of Jesus' mission:

> There is silence all around. The Baptist appears, and cries: "Repent, for the Kingdom of Heaven is at hand." Soon after that comes Jesus, and in the knowledge that He is the Coming Son of Man lays hold of the wheel of the world to set it moving on that last revolution which is to bring all ordinary history to a close. It refuses to turn, and He throws Himself upon it. Then it does turn: and crushes Him. . . . The wheel rolls onward, and the mangled body of the one immeasurably great man, who was strong enough to think of Himself as the spiritual ruler of mankind and to bend history to His purpose, is hanging upon it still. That is His victory and His reign.

This graphic synopsis reflects not only Schweitzer's renowned eschatological view of Jesus, but also the impact of Jesus' ethical vision and heroic spirit on subsequent ages, which for Schweitzer shows that there is no need of any mythological expiation to account for his greatness. The Jesus who sacrificially wrestled with the final preparations for the coming of God's Kingdom—which never came—and the Jesus who nevertheless triumphed as our spiritual ruler are one and the same. He may have been cosmologically wrong, but he was spiritually correct. Jesus' words and the biographical facts that have slowly emerged through the years of painstaking research, and the "powerful spiritual current" which still flows from both, are sufficient to reveal his special character and contribution.

Schweitzer asserts that, in addition to his profound moral sense, Jesus' uniqueness springs from his apocalypticism: "That which is eternal in the words of Jesus is due to the very fact that they are based on an eschatological world view."[4] This is not a plea for accommodating ourselves to a literal acceptance of Jesus' outmoded world view. It is a perceptive recognition of the striking effects a belief in the imminent other-worldly Reign of God had upon Jesus' whole orientation. "Jesus' achievement is that his innate and profound sense of ethics takes hold of late Jewish eschatology and expresses the hope and determination for an ethical perfection of the world."[5]

Apocalypticism usually admonishes humankind to refrain from efforts to improve present conditions, since the evil world will soon pass away. Yet in Jesus the two spheres of messianic expectation—the prophetic call of obedience to God's law *within* history, and the apocalyptic hope *beyond* history—dynamically intersect. Though he rejected this world in order to affirm a more perfect world to come, his pessimistic judgment of the temporal order did not urge him toward asceticism or withdrawal. "Jesus . . . demands that we should become free from the world, and *at the same time* that we should be active in the world." In the bedrock of early Christianity's pessimism, Schweitzer writes, there are "optimistic veins," for thanks to Jesus' unique feat, "it is not only a religion of redemption but also of the Kingdom."[6]

Although we can intellectually appreciate the fruits of historical investigations and even accept Jesus' unusual contribution to religious thought, Schweitzer cautions that bare historical facts by themselves may "help clarify . . . but never awaken spiritual life."[7] We must attempt to know Jesus not only "according to the flesh," but also "according to the spirit"—what Schweitzer terms the "spiritualized Jesus." It is not only "Jesus as historically known, but Jesus as spiritually arisen within men, who is significant for our time and can help it . . . In proportion as we have the Spirit of Jesus we have the true knowledge of Jesus." Only as we seek to obey his ethical will and enter into fellowship with the heroic spirit streaming from Him can we come to learn in our own experience and for our own time "who He is."[8]

Schweitzer writes:

> No personality of the past can be transported to the present by means of . . . affirmations about His authoritative significance. We enter into relationship with Him only by being brought together in recognition of common will, and by experiencing a clarification, enrichment, and quickening of our will through His. Thus we find ourselves again in Him. In this sense every deeper relationship between humans partakes of a mystical quality.[9]

However, those who stress the word mystical and regard the "spiritualized Jesus" solely as a hermeneutic step in the analysis underestimate the subtleties of Schweitzer's historical approach. They overlook the complexity of the historian's effort to arrive at the truth of past events. Doing so demands not only the tedious task of amassing facts, authenticating evidence and drawing careful conclusions, but the talent of creative insight as well. In order to catch the oft elusive truth, to experience "clarification and enrichment," the historian needs to enter into the multiple dimensions of the past by an empathetic in-dwelling in the subject matter itself. He or she must intuit, both factually and axiologically, the more permanent patterns in the welter of incidental particulars. This is what Schweitzer's idea of the "spiritualized Jesus" conveys. It is not a matter of abandoning historical knowledge for a mystical interpretation; it is a subtle recognition of other levels of perception.

Hence, there are implicit in Schweitzer's discussion of Jesus' significance three ways of "knowing." Speaking of his own experience metaphorically, he says that his *head* is moved by Jesus' unique conception of the Kingdom of God; his *heart* is moved by the shadowy but real person behind the words, about Whom he can say, "We know Him without knowing much about Him"; and his *hand* is moved to place itself on the plow of deed, for it is also by doing, by testing Jesus' life and words in practice, that we come to know Him. To know Jesus fully both as a recorded figure and as a living person, we must come to know him in all three ways: through rational investigation, empathetic intuition and personal action.

This approach contains no devaluation or abandonment of the historical method. But it is the religious response that, finally, becomes more important. Schweitzer dwells on the "spiritualized Jesus" because of his growing anxiety that the apocalyptic portrait disclosed by his findings might "abolish the significance of his words for our time." The historical and the religious must not be disengaged: who wishes to know Jesus as personal subject must know Him also as historical object.

Schweitzer writes,

> Whosoever preaches . . . the Gospel of Jesus must settle for himself what the *original* meaning of His sayings was, and work his way up through the *historical truth* to the eternal. During this process he will again and again have opportunity to notice that it is with this new beginning that he first truly realizes all that Jesus has to say to us, [for his] very being, that which he is and wills, manifests itself in a few of His lapidary sayings and thrusts itself upon us.[10] Anyone who ventures to look the historical Jesus straight in the face . . . knows Him as One who claims authority over him.[11]

It should be noted that he does not say, "Look the *theological* Christ in the face," for to attain the freedom which only truth can bring, Schweitzer stresses that Christianity must "reconcile itself in all sincerity with historical truth," not reconcile the historical Jesus to traditional dogmas by means of clever apologetics.

From this emerge noteworthy Schweitzerian methodological characteristics. First, Schweitzer firmly believes in the historical-critical method, applying it in all his innovative investigations, whether of Bach, Kant, Paul or Jesus. In every instance he follows the same rigorous procedure: a thorough review of the whole history of research on the topic, followed by a testing of his own hypothesis in a reconsideration of the facts. He is convinced of the importance of this objective approach, particularly for understanding the Bible.

Second, although Schweitzer knows that the New Testament is primarily a collection of faith pronouncements by evangelists and the early Church, he is convinced of the historical reliability of the oldest traditions. His *Quest* is a direct challenge to those who believe the historical is so entangled with the dogmatic that nothing clear can ever be known of Jesus, and that historical studies are otiose and must give way to a literary-imaginative reconstruction. Although the actual Jesus will always remain unknown to us in any detail, Schweitzer believes that sufficient authentic passages exist to establish trustworthy conclusions concerning his ministry.

If from a few bones paleontology can accurately reconstruct the entire skeleton of a prehistoric animal, then the same careful, painstaking procedures can and must be applied to New Testament research, if it is to regain its respected place as a historical science. The belief that there are so few fragments that no one can discover who Jesus really was can no longer be used as an excuse for resorting to the free play of theological imagination, accompanied by the implication that one is dealing with historical realities.

Third, it is strange that the first scholars systematically to employ the historical-critical method should be the very ones who come under Schweitzer's attack. But he is critical of the nineteenth century "rational" and "romantic" lives of Jesus, feeling that they were not objective enough. With very few exceptions, their authors resort to an interpretation that best suits their own theological tastes. The sophisticated reformer, whom they describe as appearing in order to establish a long-range Kingdom of Heaven on Earth, never existed. "Such a Jesus is a fiction invented by rationalism, animated by liberalism, and clad in historical garments by modern theology," Schweitzer wrote.[12] His *Quest* is a monumental testimony to these scholars' invaluable efforts, and a strong indictment of their conclusions. In their exhilaration to loosen "the bonds by which, for centuries, [Jesus] had been fettered to the rock of Church dogmatics," they set aside many of his greatest sayings and "abandoned them in a corner, like a pile of defused explosive shells," since these sayings threatened modern sensibilities. If they had been more willing to let the accounts speak in their own tongue for their own time, they would have come to a clearer understanding of Jesus.

Fourth, the eschatological passages which the scholars avoided, softened or attributed solely to the early Church are the very ones which unravel the enigmas surrounding Jesus. The early Church did not make up Jesus; it believed that he was the suffering Anointed One who would usher in the soon-to-appear Kingdom because Jesus Himself believed this. Paul interpreted Jesus' late Jewish self-understanding into a theological scheme for the Hellenistic environment.

Last, Schweitzer is convinced that his insights are the result of his objective approach to the life of Jesus, not of his personal interpretations. he believes that the facts speak for themselves and, more important, that the historical-critical approach provides not only invaluable knowledge about Christian origins, but that the facts it uncovers about Jesus serve as a basic parameter and guide to the continued clarification of our spiritual response to, and historical understanding of, Jesus for all times.

Schweitzer implies that the "canon before the canon"—the earliest witness of the apostles—not only can but must abide as the true Christian norm. Biblical authority cannot rest upon any so-called *kerygma*, for the theological-interpretive approach ultimately depends on the critical-historical. If one does not presuppose this, then the determination of the scriptural witness is either arbitrary or rests on some *extra*-scriptural authority. This means that in using the New Testament as a theological authority, the first step is *historical* rather than hermeneutical.

Schweitzer realizes the importance of keeping the historical-descriptive and the theological-interpretive methods as far apart as possible when determining facticity. We must learn what the facts are before we give mytho-poetic expression to the more enduring elements necessary for faith. Historical facts *do* make a difference—often a crucial difference, especially to a religion that regards itself as historically grounded.

The second step, the apprehension of the "spiritualized Jesus," serves as the vital link between the strictly historical and the religious imagination, where participative intuition strives to understand in depth the original occurrences.

The final step is hermeneutical. The process may begin simply in Jesus' impact on those reading the texts, but its enlivenment comes when this experience is reflected on for spiritual use. The theological response moves on a different level of insight and discovery, but it must receive its direction from the former steps.

If one understands Schweitzer's ethic of Reverence for Life and its cosmic grounding in a type of ethical vitalism, then one can see how Jesus can be, for him, "the supreme spiritual and religious authority," for Schweitzer finds the heart of this universal ethic resounding forcibly in Jesus' life and words. The universal will-to-live is an enigmatic creative-destructive force in nature, but in humankind it expresses itself mysteriously as an ethical proclivity. This will-to-love, which potentially shines in every person who comes into the world, is in Jesus turned up to its brightest illumination. For a moment we catch a glimpse of the law of love in its absolute form. The vision that a separated and alienated humanity is united in the power of rational, self-giving concern is not attained at the expense of a realistic acceptance of the world, but is, in Jesus, combined with a firm world- and life-affirmation, which is one of the necessary ingredients in Schweitzer's ethical theory. Jesus becomes for him an exemplification of the essential elements that our spiritual life demands for its success, as well as a revelatory sign of the universal will-to-love at work in the world.

In his search for the historical Jesus, Schweitzer finds that he does not have to abandon the spiritual mentor who has taken him captive since childhood. Although he can no longer accept the late Jewish titles applied to him — "Messiah," "Son of Man" or "Son of God" — and is forced to allow Jesus to remain in his own time, his scholarly investigations substantiate that Jesus' undaunted ethical will and salvific vision of a kingdom of love and justice remain a living legacy of power and insight for all times.

Notes

[1]Jurgen Moltmann, *Theology of Hope* (Harper & Row, 1967), p. 37.
[2]E.N. Mozley, *The Theology of Albert Scweitzer* (Macmillan, 1951), p. 113.
[3]Henry Clark, *The Ethical Mysticism of Albert Schweitzer* (Beacon, 1962), p. 77.
[4]Albert Schweitzer, *The Quest of the Historical Jesus* (Macmillan, 1950), p. 402.
[5]Albert Schweitzer, *Geschichte der Lebens-Jesu-Forschung*, (Mohr, 2nd ed., 1913), p. 635.
[6]Albert Schweitzer, *Christianity and the Religions of the World* (Macmillan, 1951), p. 27-29.
[7]*Geschichte*, p. 641.
[8]*Quest*, p. 401.
[9]*Geschichte*, p. 641.
[10]*Geschichte*, p. 634.
[11]Albert Schweitzer, *Out of My Life and Thought*, trans. by C.T. Campion (Holt, 1949), p. 55.
[12]*Geschichte*, p. 632.

CHAPTER FIVE

Schweitzer and Bach
From notes by Jackson Lee Ice; written by Michael Murray
1992

*Please refer to the Appendix for selections from the original notes
of Jackson Lee Ice that were the basis for this chapter.*

Albert Schweitzer was an organist and musical historian of high accomplishment. His biography of Johann Sebastian Bach and performances of Bach's music revealed to contemporary musicians and musicologists a poetic side of Bach's art not previously recognized. To this composer and this music Schweitzer felt a deep and lifelong attachment.

His love for Bach was rooted in convictions Schweitzer had formed early on about the nature of music. We shall better understand those convictions, and better understand part of the mystery of Schweitzer's personality, if we pause for a moment to glance at the past.

It is commonly accepted that music is capable of opening up to us new domains of experience, sharpening our perceptions and heightening our reactions. That it can do so with an immediacy not given to the other arts is perhaps due to its timelessness, or, more precisely, to our sense that music is somehow free of temporal limitations. Listening to a Beethoven symphony or a Mozart quartet seems to take us out of clock-time into a realm where time conforms to rhythm and tempo and can be stretched to accommodate feeling. We seem to glimpse, as it were, the everlasting. Hence the intimate relation of music to the spiritual life, and our consequent age-old use of music in church and shrine and temple.

Nor is the metaphysical quality that we perceive in music the less vital in works ostensibly secular. We may well find transcendent experience in hearing a Chopin nocturne or a Verdi opera. Indeed, such music can seem to us to reveal the Other as poignantly as a motet by Palestrina or a chorale by Luther.

The powers inherent in music have, of course, been debated by theorists and performers for hundreds of years. Even before the Greeks acknowledged that music could move the human spirit, and placed music at the service of religion, the philosophers of India and China had already done so. Confucius in particular assigned to music a role in serving the well-ordered moral universe.

Then came Plato, who regarded music as a branch of ethics and found correlations between the qualities of a human character and the qualities of the music that moved it. Then came Aristotle, who held that music could express the universal and could in itself contain truth. Aristotle declared that rhythm and melody imitate the movements of celestial bodies, delineating the music of the spheres, reflecting the moral order of the universe, and echoing the divine harmony.

In Christian times, Aquinas too saw music as reflecting divine movement and order, and as having its roots in mathematics. And Luther, who played the flute and the guitar and sang and composed hymns, considered music "one of the greatest gifts that God has given us: it is divine and therefore Satan is its enemy. For with its aid many dire temptations are overcome; the devil does not stay where music is."[1]

The debate continues to this day and has occupied such thinkers as Kant, Hegel, Schopenhauer, and Nietzsche, not to mention the distinguished philosophers of our own time. No answers have been universally agreed upon, but in general two views have continued to prevail for centuries: one holds that music is autonomous and can mean nothing more than sound and rhythm, and the other that music can and does refer to meanings other and greater than itself.

Not surprisingly, Schweitzer subscribes to the latter view, and his writings and actions all bespeak his regard for music's transcendence. He finds transcendence particularly evident in Bach, and not only in Bach's cantatas, Passions, and masses, but in the concertos, fugues, and suites. To Schweitzer, as to his friend and master Charles-Marie Widor, who penned the words in preface to Schweitzer's *J. S. Bach*, this music represents "the emotion of the infinite and the exalted" and tunes the soul "to a state in which we can grasp the truth and oneness of things, and rise above everything that is paltry, everything that divides us."[2] Or again, in the more recent words of the pianist Lorin Hollander: "Bach's music is more than high art. It is an inseparable connection between certain truths.

"I think it interesting," Hollander states,

> that those who are best in a position to understand reality—namely the particle physicists, astrophysicists and researchers into states of consciousness and transpersonal psychology—that they all look toward music. Music, after all, is the art of the vibration: the bottom line of existence as we understand it. And whether we speak of electromagnetism or the relation-

ship between light seen as a wave mechanism or light seen as a particle, somehow it points to the vibration, and to understanding life in terms of cycles. And all of this is so close to music and musical systems that we have to re-examine Pythagoras and Newton and others who saw music as something more than just a manifestation that man brought forth. They see it more that man, in his highest moments, *tapped in* to something."[3]

To communicate this transcendence was to Schweitzer the main task of the interpreter. "Bach's music depends for its effect," he writes, "not upon the perfection but upon the spirit of the performance"; for this, moreover, he believed an "inner unity of soul" was "indispensable."[4]

But although these precepts tell much about Schweitzer's sense of artistic duty, they give no clue in themselves to the action that the interpreter must take who hopes to embrace them. As a practical matter, what would Schweitzer have one do in order to gain the requisite attitude and end?

The prime imperative, as Schweitzer's own exercise of the art makes clear, is that one must banish all self-seeking and strive to be the composer's servant. It is thus essential to search out every detail of the composer's method and try to grasp every nuance of the composer's thought. Hence one must attend to every jot and tittle of the score, to every scrap of biographical information, and to the tenets of every relevant tradition—with the aim always in mind of revealing the composer's plan and obeying his will.

Here Schweitzer agrees not only with Widor and Hollander, but with many another master interpreter. For great examples suggest that the highest artistry cannot be reached unless self-expression is subordinate to duty. Think of Toscanini, who in the effort to convey the composer's meaning would add a trumpet to Beethoven's horns or violas to Debussy's violins only after scrupulous study—and a degree of soul-searching that approached the Carthusian—had persuaded him that an orchestration needed clarifying. Or take Wanda Landowska's kindred attitude toward Scarlatti or Bruno Walter's toward Bruckner. Obviously, the interpreter expresses self. But if the elements of self-expression are not to hinder the work, they must be unwitting. They must come into play only as the spontaneous result of one's inevitably being oneself and not somebody else.

In lauding this attitude, Schweitzer delineates what is a moral as well as an esthetic principle. Although he would have been the last person to deny that the good interpreter necessarily brings to bear on the work all that is best in his or her character and experience, Schweitzer is in fact proposing an ethic of self-effacement. Not for him, therefore, to ask how music might be considered ethical. To that ancient question he clearly took one answer for granted: the ethical attributes of music are found both in its innate transcendence and in the behavior required of its ablest practitioners.

If this truth can be applied to the executive artist, it seemed to him, how

much more so to the creative. Little wonder, then, that Schweitzer felt for
Bach an esteem bordering on veneration, for the greatest of all composers
was the very type of the ethical musician. "In this respect," Schweitzer
declares, Bach may well stand "highest among all creative artists; his
immense strength functioned without self-consciousness, like the forces of
nature; and for this reason it is as cosmic and copious as these."[5]

Indeed, Schweitzer found that music was for Bach an act of worship and
was therefore, in some sense, Bach's religion. To begin with, Bach cared
little whether his contemporaries understood his works. "He had put all his
devotion into them, and God at any rate certainly understood them."[6] Then
too, "Bach includes religion in the definition of art in general. All great art,
even secular, is in itself religious in his eyes; for him the tones do not perish,
but ascend to God like praise too deep for utterance."[7] And Schweitzer
recalls Bach's oft-quoted words: "Like all music, the figured bass should
have no other end and aim than the glory of God and the recreation of the
soul."[8] Accordingly, "his artistic activity and his personality are both based
on his piety. If he is to be understood from any standpoint at all, it is from
this."[9]

Schweitzer moreover concludes that though Bach was a conservative
Lutheran, his

> real religion was not orthodox Lutheranism, but mysticism .... This
> robust man, who seems to be in the thick of life with his family and his work
> ... was inwardly dead to the world. His whole thought was transfigured by
> a wonderful, serene longing for death. Again and again, whenever the text
> affords the least pretext for it, he gives voice to this longing in his music.[10]

That Bach's point of view was profoundly mystical is shown by his
treatment of every pertinent text, according to Schweitzer, and

> nowhere is his speech so moving as in the cantatas in which he discourses
> on the release from the body of this death. The Epiphany and certain bass
> cantatas are the revelation of his most intimate religious feelings. Some-
> times it is a sorrowful and weary longing that the music expresses; at others,
> a glad, serene desire, finding voice in one of those lulling cradle-songs that
> only he could write; then again a passionate, ecstatic longing, that calls
> death to it jubilantly, and goes forth in rapture to meet it .... This is Bach's
> religion as it appears in the cantatas. It transfigured his life.[11]

Whether Schweitzer's own life was transfigured by his feelings for Bach
is a matter of definition. If the specifically metaphysical connotations of the
word are set aside, the effect of Bach upon Schweitzer was certainly a kind
of transfiguration, for the persona and art of the master permeated and
enriched and transformed Schweitzer's activity. At the least, his biography

of Bach brought Schweitzer some of his earliest international acclaim and some of his most significant friendships. His recitals of Bach helped to fund the African hospital. And his knowledge of Bach doubtless reaffirmed for him the acceptability of certain character traits of his own, for both men were exceedingly strong-willed, often short-tempered, and nearly always incapable of working under the direction of persons or institutions. Both took endless pains with their work, were in large measure self-taught, and possessed an uncommon ability to see through to the heart of things. They were as well hearty in their humor, and they enjoyed vigorous good health almost to the end of their days.

But above all it was as the exemplar of ethical ideals, and as the supremely gifted musician who used his gifts in the service of God, and as the unfailing source of spiritual and intellectual refreshment that Bach personified certain truths important to Schweitzer and thus provided a locus to which Schweitzer could refer.

Nor could his admiration have been diminished by the universality of Bach's Christian message. For whether we are strictly orthodox or profoundly liberal—indeed whether we are Christian at all—it may well be Bach's sublime harmonies, rather than a discord of theologies, that at the last hour will echo in our memory of the joyous Christian dream, and bring our hearts into that dream's endurance.

Notes

[1] Martin Luther, *Gedanken über die Musik*, ed. F. A. Beck. (Berlin, 1825), p. 17.
[2] Albert Schweitzer, *J. S. Bach* (New York, 1923, vol. 1), p. xii.
[3] Private conversation, Nov. 4, 1980.
[4] Schweitzer, op.cit., vol. 2, p. 468.
[5] Ibid., vol. 1, p. 166.
[6] Ibid.
[7] Ibid., p. 167.
[8] Ibid.
[9] Ibid.
[10] Ibid., p. 169.
[11] Ibid., pp. 169-70.

CHAPTER SIX

Is "Reverence for Life" a Viable Ethic?
1981

Of the many world-renowned accomplishments of Albert Schweitzer, the one he repeatedly expressed the wish to be remembered for is his ethic of Reverence for Life. In the light of his other major contributions some might ponder the wisdom of this judgment. For despite the apparent apotheosis of his ethic by his own life, it has received, since its inception some sixty years ago, as much censure as praise. Some have found it too idealistic and impracticable; others regard it as inconsistent and provokingly vague. Even the phrase "reverence for life" appears naive to many, no more than a motto emotively employed to arouse moral sentiment, a benign rephrasing of the old love-maxim ineffectual in its lack of depth and specificity. "It has aroused much enthusiasm," observed the Danish theologian, P.G. Lindhardt, "because it can mean anything and everything."[1]

Schweitzer was not unaware of such shortcomings. Particularly when it came to satisfying the professional ethicist. "It may seem, at first glance," he wrote, "as if Reverence for Life were something too general, too lifeless to provide the content of a living ethic." But, he assures us, "anyone who comes under the influence of Reverence for Life will very soon be able to detect . . . what fire glows in its lifeless expressions."[2]

Regardless how telling the charges brought against the applicability of Schweitzer's philosophy as an ethic may be, or regardless how glowing the enthusiasm it has engendered, it can be argued that a valid evaluation of his legacy demands more than a glib dismissal or viewing his main principle as a magical incantation which will solve all moral problems. To determine "what fire glows" within his thought demands a deeper grasp of the meanings and philosophical implications of "reverence for life."

To begin with, it will help us to realize that Schweitzer is not in the strict sense an ethicist. He is less concerned with constructing a systematic ethic than with the mystery of the moral phenomenon *per se*. Actually he is more a moral prophet who seeks to expand the cognitive and moral sensitivities of the human soul in our time.

Also, one eventually discovers that Reverence for Life is not just an ethic. It includes an insight into the nature of things; it characterizes Schweiter's world-view; it is the heart of his religious philosophy. This is the reason he can say without inconsistency: "and this ethic, profound, universal, has the significance of a religion. It *is* religion."[3] And by this he also means philosophy of life. Hence his ethical discussions are ultimately entwined in an analysis of the ontological structure of man-in-the-world.

Suddenly, while straining against the "iron door" which barred him from discovering the basic principal of the moral, and stumbling about the dense "thickets" of pessimism searching for a path that would lead him, with intellectual honesty, toward a type of cosmic affirmation, there flashed upon him a phrase that fused together in a natural and logical way existence and value, nature and spirit, the "is" and the "ought," world- and life-affirmation in one epiphanic insight. The two essential features of the religious life—ethical involvement and cosmic rootedness—must, he realized, be united in a natural way. Man and nature, reason and reality, must not be joined either falsely by equating them, or by regarding them as mutually exclusive. A way must be discerned as to how, and to what extent, they are involved in each other. The value proclivities of humankind, including the ethical, must not be left dangling subjectively without their objective counterparts; and the necessity of world rootedness must not be gained at the expense of intellectual integrity nor existential involvement. With his insight of "reverence for life," which flashed upon his mind "unforeseen and unsought," Schweitzer believed he had found the philosophical solution.

The problem which challenged Schweitzer was not to construct a code of fixed ethical procedures superseding all past theories, but to discover a *Humanitatsphilosophie* which was both world as well as life-affirming, a religious outlook which bound logically into a living unity both the mystical-sacramental and the empirical-social elements. This is no simple task. But that he was successful in moving toward this goal can partially be seen in the following analysis of the multiple meanings—descriptive as well as prescriptive—of the phrase.

First, as a biological expression, "reverence for life" means I am an urge to survival. I instinctively affirm my own life by reason of the fact that I am a body that wills to stay alive. Schweitzer calls this an "instinctive reverence for life." With every beat-beat-beat of one's heart, there is an unconscious affirmation of life within us. Schweitzer is quite explicit about ethics being rooted in humankind's nature. Reverence for life, he writes, "does not need to make any pretensions to high titles nor noble sounding theories to explain its existence. Quite simply, it has the courage to admit that it comes about through physiological make-up. It is given physically. But the point is that it can arrive at the noblest spirituality."[4]

Secondly, I also consciously revere my own life. As a self-aware organism I seek to develop my own powers. I am also will-to-self-realization. Purposive self-development of course, comes only when I move from a "simple" to a "deepened" self-affirmation, from an unconscious to a more aware self-regard. "How this striving originated within us, and how it has developed, we do not know, but it is given with our existence. We must act upon it, if we would not be unfaithful to the mysterious will-to-live which is within us."[5] Thus, "reverence for life" characterizes the discovery of what it means to respect myself and to realize my own life-giving potentialities. A lack of respect for ourselves makes us our own worst enemies. This meaning of Schweitzer's term is often overlooked.

Thirdly, the phrase signifies not only an instinctive survival urge or urge to realize my own potentialities, but also a proclivity toward love and concern. I am also will-to-relatedness. I desire to enter into and be part of others' lives. This describes my being as accurately as my tendency to fight to stay alive or selfishly to seek my own happiness. It is the phase in the development of the human being when the tendential regard and concern for "the other" is refined and enhanced.

We must not be naive as to what Schweitzer is about here. The will-to-live is not transmuted automatically into an altruistic will-to-love. The warring ego is not replaced. There is in our natures both a will-to-self-preservation and a will-to-concern. That persons have a certain nature does not *ipso facto* mean that all their potentialities will be completely or properly realized. Humans' concern for others is not lifted to an altruistic level without effort, will and sensitivity. It is the task of elemental thought, speaking out of the momentary but natural impulse of pity and sympathy, to refine and to raise the will-to-relatedness to the level of moral concern for others. "This reverence for life," says Schweitzer, "is given as an element of my will-to-live and becomes clearly conscious of itself only as I reflect about my life and about the world."[6]

There are two aspects of the will-to-relatedness which I discovered that must be mentioned: the active and the passive.

Active, or moral, relatedness exhibits itself dually: in humans' gregariousness and need to belong—which issue in the rise of societies and solidary interests; and in their need to love and to be loved—which issue in ties of friendship, sympathetic concern and moral responsibility.

Passive, or cosmic, relatedness also expresses itself in two ways: namely, as the need for union in a wider, more universal sense—which issues mainly in man's religious, and quasi-religious, expressions signified by the search of the holy, or wholeness, and at-one-ment; and as the will-to-meaning which issues in humanity's intellectual quests for truth concerning the nature of things and his possible relations to them, for knowledge is a form of relatedness. Reverence for life means reverence for truth: another neglected meaning of Schweitzer's term.

It is interesting to note that Schweitzer insists we fail to fulfill our wills-to-relatedness if they are accomplished only in a passive, purely intellectual, or mystical manner. As we cannot be satisfied to belong to the universe only as physical objects, so we cannot be related meaningfully to it only intellectually as calculating machines. Knowledge of external relations is not enough; we also need knowledge of internal relatedness. The crucial point to remember, however, is that for Schweitzer our knowledge of the world at this juncture becomes a special kind of knowledge that only an active existential participation can bring. This is what he means when he insists that our world-view (passive relatedness) must be based upon our life-view (active relatedness).

In the fourth place, "reverence for life" means an instinctive concern, not only for my own life or for other human life, but for all life whatsoever. It is obvious Schweitzer does not confine the "will-to-live" or "life" to the human level; it encompassed all organisms. Indeed, not only does it describe the animate, it applies to the inanimate as well: the will-to-live is found even "in the flowering tree, the strange forms of the medusa, in the blade of grass, in the crystal."[7]

Regardless how fleeting this feeling of empathy and concern may be, it is felt in all of us from time to time. There is a chthonic link with the will-to-live which we perceive in all animal, bird, fish, insect and even plant life. This gives Schweitzer's ethic its total inclusiveness when he moves from the purely descriptive to the prescriptive use of the phrase. Schweitzer makes the prophetic comment that future ages will look back upon our period of history with amazement for our neglect to include such life within the sphere of moral behavior, just as we look back in disbelief at those who once regarded the non-white peoples as less developed forms of human life.

Fifthly, giving ontological status to the term "life," or "will-to-live," the phrase "reverence for life" becomes a capsulized expression for Schweitzer's "mysticism of reality" or religious philosophy. It signifies humanity's widest relatedness. Everything is part of an amazing and enigmatic enterprise; everything is "in the grasp of the inexplicable forward urging Will in which all Being is grounded."[8] This meaning directs our attention, not just to socio-biological life, as if this were the only true source of our existence and concern, but to reality in its widest, fullest, deepest sense.

A clarification must be interjected at this point. Schweitzer's words at times convey the impression that man and the world are essentially alike, united felicitously under the aegis of some Universal Moral Will or Benevolent Power. But this is not so. He is adamant on this point. Humankind has yearned to attain to this idealistic rationale of the universe, but such a philosophical world-view is specious. According to Schweitzer it is impossible to read into the physical world an overall optimistic *telos* or moral purpose. The will-to-live cannot be traced alike in all its traits from the lowest to the highest levels, for "high up in the ascent it breaks off with chasms ahead." There is seemingly a division of the will-to-live against itself: life feeds on life; there is senseless pain and waste; nature is destructive as well as constructive. The first two meanings of "reverence for life" do give us a firm tie with their cosmic counterparts apparently, but when we approach the place where we may validly find moral and rational activity in the world-at-large with which we may identify ourselves, the facts fail us. Outside us the will-to-live is an enigmatic, creative and destructive force; only within us does it manifest itself as an aware, concerned will-to-ethical relatedness. This is why Schweitzer insists that in order to attain a system of thought which unites both value and existence, our world-view (cosmic relatedness) must be based upon our life-view (moral relatedness) and not *vice versa*. But this does not mean, however, a leaving behind or departing from experience, facts and the outer dimension of our reality.

Hence the fifth meaning of "reverence for life" signifies a veneration for the Universal Will in which all life is grounded. Through this attitude humanity seeks to become united with the Cosmic Will and to overcome in some small way the puzzling estrangement (*Selbstentsweiung*) between the creative-destructive force without and the creative will-to-love within.

Finally, in the obvious meaning of the term, "reverence for life" serves as an ethical admonition or moral maxim by stressing what one ought to do. This is its prescriptive function.

It is interesting that Schweitzer is able to combine in a natural way the "is" and the "ought" in one expression. Each of the descriptive meanings has, at the same time, its prescriptive overtone, which arises as a puzzling but essential feature of the human phenomenon. It is our essential, or potential nature, speaking to our actual, conditioned nature. I instinctively revere my own life—I "ought" to develop my potential as a person in the highest manner possible; I have a natural tendency toward concern for others—I "ought" to love others and devote myself to them more; I have a natural kinship with all living things—I "ought" to show more concern and tenderness toward them; I have a natural tendency toward world-relatedness—I "ought" to seek to become united through thought and moral deeds with the mysterious Universal Will in which all Being, all will-to-live, is grounded. Thus Schweitzer's moral "ought" and "world-affirmation" spring from the very heart of an analysis of the nature of man-in-the-world; both burgeon from the same root stalk.

Reverence for Life characterizes and energizes a total existential outlook by combining the mystical and the practical, theory and practice, self and the world. This is its main value. It may fail those who demand a complete moral program of maxims and means which can be plugged easily into our existing mores and legal systems, but it succeeds as an attempt to synthesize in one basic outlook and principle the essential features which reason requires of an honest and viable religious philosophy of life. Schweitzer has demonstrated that deep religious convictions are not incompatible with thought, and that ethical values are not incompatible with facts.

Reverence for Life offers us, then, not a final word, a finished philosophy, but a beginning point, a foundation for formulating multiple lifestyles that will guide humanity toward future fulfillment in accordance with a vague and simple, but a powerful and imperious universal mandate, one ingrained into our very natures. Whether or not humanity moves to future plateaus of further accomplishments might possibly depend upon those individuals who exhibit a profound and continuing "reverence for life" in the full ethical, ecological, religious and philosophical sense of the phrase.

Now, at least, we can better understand Schweitzer's enthusiasm over the epiphany that came to him on Gabon's Ogowe River in 1915, as well as his wish that he be remembered for this achievement above all else.

Notes

[1] P. G. Lindhardt, *Albert Schweitzer: A Study of his Philosophy of Life*, (London, 1960), p. 121.

[2] Albert Schweitzer, *Out of My Life and Thought*, trans. C.T. Campion (New York: Holt, 1961), p. 232.

[3] Albert Schweitzer, *Philosophy of Civilization*, trans. C.T. Campion (New York: Macmillan, 1959), p. 309.

[4] Henry Clark, "The Ethic of Reverence for Life," *The Ethical Mysticism of Albert Schweitzer.* (Boston: Beacon Press, Inc., 1962), Appendix 1, pp. 182-183.

[5] Albert Schweitzer, *Kultur Und Ethik.* (Munich: Biederstain Verlag, 1948), p. 210.

[6] Schweitzer, *Philosophy of Civilization*, p. XV.

[7] Ibid, p. 282.

[8] Ibid.

CHAPTER SEVEN

The Ecological Crisis: Radical Monotheism vs. Schweitzer's Ethical Pantheism

1975

The growing ecological crisis which threatens the industrial nations of the world is now so obvious that it seems a matter of supererogation to mention it.[1] The problem is no longer something statistically abstract and remote, but is disturbingly real and near. We are at last painfully aware of the pervasive and sinister changes which our ravaging of the earth's irreplaceable resources and our progressive polluting of the environment with fouling wastes and genocidal chemicals have wrought. Now we are reaping the fruits of irremediable damage from seeds sown solely in unconcern with an eye to immediate profit and gratification. Not only have we callously upset the unity and balance of nature; we have also, by indiscriminate testing of monstrous nuclear weapons, wantonly tampered with the genetic heritage of the whole human family—spoiling the earth for ourselves and posterity. Such blatant malpractice, we have discovered, brings its own bitter and frightening rewards.

How did we arrive at such a juncture?

I

The answer which comes immediately to mind is that this malaise is due mainly to human greed. But this is only partially true. Modern humanity is neither more nor less greedy than its ancestors. The only difference, perhaps, is that now its greed is covertly sanctioned by a national economic theory—whether it is called capitalism or communism—and by an egregious patriotism which sanctions any act as right if it is done in the interest of national security. Greed is merely one factor among others.

Our ecological dilemma is part of a larger and deeper crisis. It did not suddenly appear as a seasonal blight on the branches of Western culture; it has a long history, and its causes are deep in its roots. It is one of the symptoms, not the cause, of our present problems. It belongs to the general decay of culture foreseen by so many outstanding thinkers, such as Albert Schweitzer, who raised their voices in warning over half a century ago.

While interned as a prisoner of war in France in 1914, Schweitzer wrote: "We are living today under the sign of the collapse of civilization."[2] In this book, originally entitled *The Decay and the Restoration of Civilization*, he makes a penetrating study of the diseases which were slowly dissolving the foundations of Western Culture. His symptomatology identifies such causes as: (a) the dominance of the market-oriented way of life; (b) the mistaking of national interests for universal values; (c) the rise of aggressive imperialism, with its cry of "blood and soil"; (d) the over-specialization in all fields of thought which has truncated man's humanity and narrowed his vision; (e) the over-organization and predatory control of human life with their subordination of the human to the technological, of the individual to the state, and of nature to industry.

Superseding and overarching these specific causes is the more fundamental cause which Schweitzer describes as the collapse of the ethical and optimistic *Weltanschauung* of the West which marks the eventual waning of civilizing ideas, humanizing goals and universal ethical principles. The ideals of our Judeo-Christian-Humanistic culture have become a thin, superficial cosmetic behind which lurks a confused, amoral and pessimistic face.

All these causes—specific and general—are linked both directly and indirectly to our present crisis in ecology. Schweitzer's insight is profound when he ultimately derives many of the underlying causes for our "time of troubles" from our basic world-view, that unseen, ubiquitous backdrop against which and according to which we see and mold ourselves and our world.

But this is most puzzling. How (we well may ask), with so much success, so many advances in every field, and so many values accruing to our superior way of life, could the Industrial Revolution, the rise of science, democratic laissez-faire ideals, and the triumph of supertechnology lead us so astray? Why do they seem insidiously to contain the seeds of their own destruction, so that the harder we work for "progress" and "success," the harder we work for our demise?

Strange and disturbing as it may seem, many facets of our present crisis have their beginnings in the Bible. For example, our ecological miseries actually go back to the time when Christianity finally triumphed over the pagan world and was accepted as the one and only, divinely sanctioned world-view. With the eventual dominance of monotheism over pantheism, the dedivinization of Nature occurred together with the acceptance of a belief and attitude which were invidiously to color our relations to nature. From the advent of Christianity onward, humankind's habitat was no longer Mother Earth who mysteriously nurtured and sustained her children. The world was no longer filled with deities, no more the abode of the gods. Mount Olympus became only a pile of dead rock. A radical bifurcation finally triumphed, and all earth's creatures, places and things were ultimately desacralized.

Humanity's close kinship with earth used to hold in check its greedy impulse to exploit nature, but monotheism disturbed the balance between humankind and nature; the umbilical cord was severed; the mirror of Nature was broken.

Both Christian monotheism and secular atheism are imbued with the same taint, the same false split between God and nature and (it logically follows) between humankind and nature. Secular atheism is merely an extension of this encompassing world-view, carrying its implication of humankind's arrogant dominance over "lifeless matter" to its extreme.

Secondly, our ecological troubles derive also from the acceptance of the mytho-poetic vision of God giving humans dominion over all things upon the earth: "over the fish of the sea, and over the fowl of the air, and over every living thing that moveth upon the earth." Nature was divinely relegated to a subordinate position as raw material to be subdued and conquered. This desacralized view of plant, insect, and animal life became an inextricable part of Western people's attitude—so much so that they take it today as a matter of course. No wonder that any alternative view which calls for the tempering of humankind's exploitive acts with mystical concern for Nature and her creatures is considered silly. No wonder that any protest, in the names of sanity and reverence, against manufacturers polluting our rivers and lakes, against land developers tearing up the land, or against hunters "for fun and sport" causing needless suffering to our wildlife, is strangely ineffectual: their mindscapes have been formed for centuries by a vitiated version of the cooperative mutuality of human beings and nature. Nature's role in humankind was eclipsed by Christianity's idolatrous view of humankind's role in nature.

The third contributing religious cause of the ecological crisis is the West's succumbing to a literal eschatological hope which looks toward the end of the natural world and the supernatural coming of a new heaven and earth. This is the belief, so strongly a hidden part of our secular interpretation of "history" and "progress," in the Judeo-Christian prophecy of the inevitable passing away of the world. This supposedly is the triumph of God over the world, of good over evil, of spirit over flesh, of mind over matter—or, in secular terms, of supertechnology over nature. By the end of the age the world, condemned by God since the Fall like an old tenement house, will be worn and used up, so why bother with its care? Earth is merely a stopping place, a testing ground, a shadowy vale of tears, a material stepping-stone to a higher spiritual realm, or a disposable mechanical asteroid.

This continues to be a powerfully pervasive reinforcement of humanity's attitude that the earth is for its own use however it sees fit, that nature is nonsacred, and that matter is only so much dead stuff to be pragmatically shoveled about.

Human beings, of course, need hope for the future. Their very nature and existence demand it. But when that hope diminishes the essential importance and sacredness of their present home and their fellow creatures, it becomes a false hope deleterious to their life and health—both physical and spiritual —here and now.

The fourth reason Western culture is facing an ecological crisis, one that is logically related to the causes cited above, is due to the Christian belief in nonnatural, nonprogressive revelation. It is the conviction that God spoke once and for all through the Bible and that no new or further divine knowledge needs to be, or can be, known. No new authoritative insights about God, man, nature, or their interrelationship, are possible. God and the prophets stopped revealing eighteen hundred years ago. Therefore Christianity resisted, and still resists, any changes in religious outlook or basic beliefs which may help us face the new and demanding problems of our present age of anguish. We can only depend upon religious thinkers to rechurn old inadequacies and to lull us into satisfaction with ingenious variations on past theological themes.

The belief that Christianity embodies the ultimate world-view which can meet any new or unforseen challenge or problem is arrogantly myopic. The promise that it can continually bring "new treasures out of old" is grossly misleading; in any ultimate sense it is illusory. Out of old treasure one gets old treasure. Sundry novel combinations may appear, but they are of the same basic material. What is urgently needed is the discovery of new pearls of wisdom and as yet unmined veins of gold; riches that the treasure-houses of orthodox Christianity and Judaism do not contain.

The last cause of our technological nightmare arising from the Christian impact upon the Western world-view is the reinforcement and ultimate sanction of capitalism's insatiable thirst for material gains by the Protestant ethic and its scheme of salvation. Protestantism gave the rising capitalistic spirit of the eighteenth and nineteenth centuries a metaphysical and religious world-view which fit like hand in glove. Eventually, this voracious economic way of life became a pseudo-religion for the industrial nations of the world, unfortunately bereft more and more of the humanizing safeguards of the Christian ethic and its guiding, critical precepts. Western humanity's heart was set solely upon amassing material influence at any price. And verily it has its reward.

Whether these trends were the result of an accurate rendering or a faulty exegesis of the Bible, whether directly deduced from theological statements or only psychologically derived, whether due to "true" teaching or to "sinful" practice, makes little difference. The thrust of orthodox Christianity culturally engendered a world-view which was to issue in these beliefs that have become so ecologically deleterious.

What steps can be taken to avert further disaster? Or perhaps the question should be phrased in religious terms: What must we do to be saved?

II

The nemesis we have brought on ourselves cannot be dispelled by relying on the same conceptual tools. Redoubling our technological effort when we have myopic aims is futile. The stock-in-trade messiahs—capitalistic Christianity, Communism, scientific humanism—cannot extricate modern industrial humanity from this present plight. What it needs is a change of sensibility and world-consciousness, and this demands experiences and efforts of a philosophical or religious nature. As Lynn White, Jr., writes: "Both our present science and our present technology are so tinctured with orthodox Christian arrogance toward nature that no solution for our ecological crisis can be expected from them alone. Since the roots of our trouble are so largely religious, the remedy must also be essentially religious."[3] We must strive to become reintegrated with the whole of nature from which we have become estranged. We can do this in at least two ways: first, by expanding our concept of God or World Spirit; and, second, by enlarging the Christian ethic.

This means, initially, that we must temper our harsher sentiments nurtured by a radical monotheism with the more tender, vivifying, and unifying spirit expressed in the pantheistic religions.[4] The Christian conception of God as a wholly transcendent Being over and against us must be modified by the conception of God as both immanent and transcendent, a Power that is with us more than in spirit alone, infused into and strangely and marvelously identifiable with matter and flesh also. This would resacralize the world and bring our theological beliefs more into line with our ecological knowledge.

Nature is reminding us of the obvious fact that we are not masters of our environment to the singular, isolated extent we prefer to believe. She is ominously demonstrating that the prideful use of power to subdue all things beneath the yoke of human domination is disastrous, making us not masters but victims. Life, as the pantheistic religions intuitively foresaw, is a cooperative venture to a greater extent than we ever realized. It is time we strove more to become members of nature instead of manipulators of matter. The cruder forms of power which Western humanity has exhibited over the past two hundred years must be tempered with the more enduring and life-giving powers of concern, love and reverence. This is the true nature of divine power—as expressed by the Christ, the Buddha and the Bodhisattvas. The less aggressive religions, such as Shinto, Confucianism, Taoism and the American Indian religions, which teach the harmony of humankind with Nature and stress noninterference with her sacred ways, perhaps possess the world-view now offering the strongest hope for saving humankind from its present dilemma.

Albert Schweitzer, who prophetically exhibited in his life and thought so many of the turmoils and challenges our era was to face, and evidenced extraordinary advance perception of its needs, wrote: "I could never get beyond . . . the conflict between theism and pantheism but allowed them to stand as an unsolved struggle in my soul."[5] Schweitzer's religious philoso-phy of Reverence for Life is compatible with the subtle types of pantheism our radical monotheism needs: a religion which sees all things "in the grasp of the infinite, inexplicable, forward urging will in which all Being is grounded."[6]

> The fear that Christianity originating in this thought will step into a crass pantheism is unreal. Every form of living Christianity is pantheistic in that it is found to envisage everything that exists as having its being in the great First Cause of all being . . . . Therein it does not stand in opposition to pantheism but emerges together with it as the ethically determined out of what is natural and undetermined.[7]

"My philosophy," wrote Schweitzer, " has developed into an ethical pantheism, the inevitable synthesis of theism and pantheism."[8]

This leads to the second step of the solution—the ethic of Reverence for Life, which in Schweitzer's words is "the ethic of love widened into universality." It is the ethic of Jesus, raised to a universal level of thought, made cosmic in scope, and "recognized as a logical consequence of thought."[9]

Is it not strange that the ethic of Jesus concerns itself only with the relation of person to person and says nothing of any love or compassion we ought to have for other sentient creatures and all life around us of which we are so much a part and upon which we utterly depend for our very lives? Schweitzer also considered this a peculiar deficiency in Judeo-Christian thought.

> It was quite incomprehensible to me—this was before I began going to school—why in my evening prayers I should pray for human beings only.

So when my mother had prayed with me and had kissed me good night, I used to add silently a prayer that I had composed myself for all living creatures: "Dear God, protect and bless all living things; keep them from evil and let them sleep in peace."[10]

How often Schweitzer has been ridiculed as a sentimental old fool for going out of his way to not kill or injure a worm on the path, the ants by his door, and the mosquito on his sleeve; for taking time in his overworked schedule to care for the sick and useless forest creatures brought to him by the natives; for moving trees to another location instead of cutting them down; for calling himself a mass murderer of bacteria and the persecutor of the mice in his house! It is difficult enough to love one's neighbor, much less one's enemies; but to enlarge our ethical duty to include animal, insect and plant life seems positively ludicrous. But now we wonder. Is the Christian ethic, as Schweitzer maintained, too narrow in its scope? Are we now forced by our circumstances and the facts brought to light by the ecological sciences to enlarge Jesus' commands to encompass all life? Must we do this not only to survive but to be truly moral? Does God's plan include *all* things, not just humans? The ecological crisis has transformed the derisive smile we once had for such ideas into sober reflection.

Schweitzer perceptively observed:

> It is the fate of every truth to be an object of ridicule when it is first acclaimed. It was once considered foolish to suppose that black men were really human beings and ought to be treated as such. What was once foolish has now become a recognized truth. Today it is considered as exaggeration to proclaim constant respect for every form of life as being the serious demand of a rational ethic. But the time is coming when people will be amazed that the human race existed so long before it recognized that thoughtless injury to life is incompatible with real ethics. Ethics is in its unqualified form extended responsibility with regard to everything that has life.[11]

And according to Schweitzer, not only animals and insects, plants and trees, but also viruses and crystals, are imbued with the will to live. All things on earth are sacred to him and each in its own way comes under the aegis of his ethic of Reverence for Life.

> There slowly grew up in me an unshakable conviction that we have no right to inflict suffering and death on another living creature unless there is some unavoidable necessity for it, and that we ought all of us to feel what a horrible thing it is to cause suffering and death out of mere thoughtlessness. And this conviction has influenced me only more and more strongly with time. I have grown more and more certain that at the bottom of our hearts we all think this, and that we fail to acknowledge it and to carry our belief into practice chiefly

because we are afraid of being laughed at by other people as sentimentalists, though partly also because we allow our best feelings to get blunted. But I vowed that I would never let my feelings get blunted and that I would never be afraid of the reproach of sentimentalism.[12]

He continues:

A man is really ethical only when he obeys the constraint laid on him to help all life which he is able to succor, and when he goes out of his way to avoid injuring anything living. He does not ask how this or that life deserves sympathy as valuable in itself, nor how far it is capable of feeling. To him life as such is sacred. He shatters no ice crystal that sparkles in the sun, tears no leaf from the tree, breaks off no flower, and is careful not to crush any insect as he walks.[13]

Ordinary ethics seeks to find limits within the sphere of human life and relationships. But the absolute ethics of the will to live must reverence every form of life, seeking so far as possible to refrain from destroying any life, regardless of its particular type. It says of no instance of life, "This has no value.[14]

But man comes again and again into the position of being able to preserve his own life and life generally only at the cost of other life. If he has been touched by the ethic of reverence for life, he injures and destroys life *only under a necessity which he cannot avoid*, and never from thought-lessness. So far as he is a free man he uses every opportunity of tasting the blessedness of being able to assist life and avert it from its suffering and destruction.[15]

What the Industrial Revolution did in the nineteenth century to men, women and children—treating them as expendable surplus commodities to feed the machines of big business—the twentieth century is doing to nature. As the rights of the underprivileged classes grew out of this earlier conflict (and are still being fought for against infractions by their exploiters), let us hope that the divine rights of nature and all that lives may arise out of the present crisis; that we may gain a new level of ethical and religious consciousness: not as the result of sentimentalism but as the result of an inner logical necessity. Just as we have discovered "Love thy neighbor" is no sentimental shibboleth of bleeding hearts but a basic biological law, not merely for individual survival but for fulfillment of the species, so may the ethic of Reverence for Life eventually be recognized to be founded on a basic law of nature. It is one of the great achievements of Schweitzer's ethic that it combines in a natural and logical way the "is" and the "ought," "fact" and "value," the "descriptive" and the "prescriptive." Reverence for Life is not superimposed *on* nature but is empirically drawn *from* it. The facts of the physical world are dictating a moral "ought." It is no longer a moralistic option but a vital necessity: "Have ethical responsibility and compassion for all *life*—or die!" This is not merely good ethics, it is sound ecology; and it is the fuller vision of the truly enlightened and religious person.

The ethical pantheism of Schweitzer and the panpsychism of process philosophy may be the next steps upward in humanity's vision of God which will lift it above the limitations of radical monotheism and beyond the present ecological crisis. For as Teilhard de Chardin, the French priest-scientist, so prophetically wrote: "The world will not be converted to the heavenly promise of Christianity unless Christianity has previously been converted to the promise of the earth."

Notes

[1]This study was occasioned not only by my studies of Schweitzer's ecological ethic of Reverence for Life, but also by the provocative essay "The Genesis of Pollution" by Arnold J. Toynbee in *Horizon*, Summer, 1973, whose ideas I comment upon and expand.

[2]Albert Schweitzer, *The Philosophy of Civilization* (New York: Macmillan, 1949), p. 1.

[3]Lynn White, Jr., "The Historical Roots of Our Ecological Crisis," *Science*, 155 (1967), pp. 1203-7.

[4]The term "radical monotheism" as used here refers to a belief in radical transcendence which appears in forms of theistic absolutism or supernaturalism and does not necessarily signify the meanings made popular by H. Richard Niebuhr in his book *Radical Monotheism and Western Culture* (New York: Harper, 1960).

[5]Oskar Kraus, *Albert Schweitzer: His Work and His Philosophy* (London: A. & C. Black, 1944), pp. 42-43.

[6]Schweitzer, *Philosophy of Civilization*, p. 283.

[7]Albert Schweitzer, *Out of My Life and Thought* (New York: Holt, 1949), pp. 238-39.

[8]Kraus, *Albert Schweitzer*, p. 73.

[9]Schweitzer, *Life and Thought*, p. 232.

[10]Albert Schweitzer, *Memories of Childhood and Youth* (New York: Macmillan, 1950), p. 40.

[11]Schweitzer, *Philosophy and Civilization*, p. 310-11.

[12]Schweitzer, *Childhood and Youth*, p. 31.

[13]Schweitzer, *Philosophy of Civilization*, p. 310.

[14]Albert Schweitzer, "The Ethics of Reverence for Life," *Christendom*, Winter, 1936, p. 233.

[15] Schweitzer, *Life and Thought*, p. 234, (italics mine).

CHAPTER EIGHT

Schweitzer: An 18th Century Anachronism?

From notes by Jackson Lee Ice; compiled by M. Marie Ice

1992

Schweitzer felt it was imperative that we bring into focus the concept of natural law and the inalienable rights of humankind, as was done, according to him, in the eighteenth and early nineteenth centuries. This age sought for "a living concept of law." It is also for this reason that Schweitzer stood as a champion of these periods of history.

In order to understand more clearly his position on this subject, I wish to present his reasons why he believed the eighteenth century was to be "the greatest epoch in the history of human civilization,"[1] for in these citations there is brought out the importance of, and the close relation which exists in his mind between ethics, religion, social and political reforms, human rights, and natural law.

First, it possessed an optimistic-ethical world-view which allowed the "belief-in-progress" and the "will-to-progress" full play. It was the type of world outlook in which existed " . . . the unshaken confidence that nothing can delay the speedy and conclusive victory of the purposive and moral."[2] The outstanding minds of the age had a deep trust in the power of reason to unveil the mysteries of the universe and guarantee for humankind a better existence; and it was upon this foundation that they built their ideals and were capable of drawing the confidence and inspiration necessary for their realization. "Thanks to the fully worked out optimistic-ethical world-view with which the belief in progress is environed in the course of the eighteenth century, these generations prove capable of thinking out the ideals of civilization and advancing towards their realization."[3] "In those departments of life in which the important matter is the shaping of thought according to ideals given by reason . . . they are as creative as any generation ever has been."[4] It is because of their reverence for truth, their confidence in reason, their faith in creating a new era for all humankind, and their endeavors to broaden ethics to affect every sphere of activity, that Schweitzer praised this epoch in history.

This optimistic-ethical outlook, which brought all areas of human endeavor under the scrutiny and control of enlightened reason, resulted in outstanding accomplishments and reforms. To religion it was a cathartic experience.

> That religion should be split up into various antagonistic confessional bodies is to them an offense against reasonable reflection. Only relative, not absolute, authority, they maintained, can be allowed to the belief which is handed down in historical formulas. Finding exression in so many and such varied forms it can, of course, be nothing but a more or less imperfect expression of the ethical religion taught by reason, which must be equally intelligible to all men. The right thing is, therefore, to strive after the religion of reason, and to accept as true only such parts of the various confessions as are in harmony with it.[5]

The development of the "religion of reason" fostered a period of toleration between different denominations and religions; it led to the historical study of religions and to the critical analysis of religious creeds and beliefs. The idea of a universal religion took root.

> Again, the will-to-progress of the eighteenth century makes as clean a sweep of nationalist as of religious prejudices. Above and beyond individual nations it points to mankind as the great object towards which ideals are to be directed. Educated people accustom themselves to see in the State not so much an organ of national feeling as a mere organization for legal and economic purposes. Cabinets may carry on war with each other, but in the thought of the common people there grows up a recognition of the brotherhood of nations.[6]
>
> The education of mankind in citizenship makes splendid progress. The general good becomes the criterion of excellence both for the commands of rulers and the obedience of their subjects, while at the same time a beginning is made towards securing that everyone shall be educated in a manner corresponding to his human dignity and the needs of his personal welfare. The war against ignorance is begun.[7]
>
> In the sphere of law, too, the will-to-progress acquires strength. The ideas of Hugo Grotius find acceptance. The law of reason is exalted in the convictions of the men of the eighteenth century to a position above all traditional maxims of jurisprudence. It alone is allowed to have a permanent authority, and legal decisions have to be in harmony with it. Fundamental principles of law, principles everywhere equally beyond dispute, have to be deduced from human nature. To protect these and thus ensure to every human being a human value with an inviolable measure of freedom of which he can never be robbed, is the first task of the State.[8]

The eighteenth century also "waged war against superstition." It obtained recognition for humanity in the eyes of the law. Torture was abolished, first in Prussia in the year 1740 through a cabinet order of Frederick the Great. (Also, "in 1740 the philosopher and jurist of Halle, Christian Thomarius, published his essays condemning trial for witchcraft, and about the middle of the century the law courts in most of the States of Europe refused to concern themselves any longer with the crime of magic."[9]) It was demanded of the individual that he should place himself to the service of the community. English emigrants formulated in America for the first time the rights of man. The ideal of humanity began to gain significance. ("Side by side with the fight against absence of law and the existence of inhuman laws, go efforts to adapt law to circumstances. Bentham raises his voice against laws which tolerate usury, against senseless customs duties, and against inhuman methods of colonization."[10]) People dared to grasp the thought that lasting peace must reign on earth. Kant wrote a book on "Everlasting Peace," and in it represented the thought that even politics must submit to the principles of ethics. Finally came the abolition of slavery, an achievement brought about by the spirit of the eighteenth century.[11]

"Thanks to belief in progress, new life streams into ethics. The inner relations between ethics and world- and life-affirmation begin to take effect. The elementary impulses to activity which are embodied in the Christian ethic are set free, and belief in progress gives them an aim: the transformation of the circumstances of society and of mankind."[12]

"The religious-ethical spirit of the eighteenth century desired then to make the Kingdom of God a reality on earth."[13]

These are some of the poignant reasons why Schweitzer extolled the worthiness of the Enlightenment period. To him its accomplishments far outweigh its defects. "Only a world-view which accomplishes all that rationalism did has a right to condemn rationalism. The greatness of that philosophy is that its hands are blistered."[14]

It is understandable why Schweitzer possessed an inordinate fondness for this period of history. The results he has listed speak for themselves. It was an era in which the "triadic essence of civilization" (religion, philosophy, and ethics) was a strong and active force within society. Yet one wonders whether Schweitzer was not so intoxicated by these particular attributes of the age that he forgot that the eighteenth century was also an age in which there grew philosophical, economic, political and social theories which are antipodal to Schweitzer's views, and which, if they did not initiate, at least gave impetus to materialism, subjectivism, relativism, hedonism, utilitarianism and the discrediting and loss of confidence in the religious world-view. It is justifiable to select from the philosophies and accomplishments of the Illuminati of the *Aufklarung* just those which are asymptotic to one's own views, but to rest a decision that it is the "greatest epoch in the history of human civilization" on these choices alone, and ignoring other movements, trends, influences and thinkers which were as important and outstanding, is an invalid procedure of evaluation.

> His esteem of the eighteenth century is a weak argument: fortunately, his ethic is in no way affected by this judgment; but the eulogy does appear to justify the criticism that his historical analysis is akin to this theological scheme, a drawing in black and white, lacking in shades, failing to list the evils which then prevailed.[15]

Also, it is questionable whether the many laudable accomplishments were due *solely* to the operation of an optimistic-ethical world-view, as Schweitzer indicated. There were many intellectual forces at work at that time, not to mention the other multifarious and subtle influences which played upon the lives and conditions of the enlightened peoples.[16] Sorokin writes,

> I find especially peculiar Schweitzer's particularly high estimate of the Stoic *Weltanschauvngen* and the philosophical, ethical, political, economic and social theories of the seventeenth and especially the eighteenth centuries . . . . He seems to be quite unaware of the shortcomings of these theories. . . . [which] if they did not initiate . . . , at least gave a great impetus to, an ethical and civilizational decay which became catastrophic . . . at the middle of the nineteenth century . . . . For me this exceptionally high evaluation of these theories by Schweitzer is entirely incomprehensible.[17]

Perhaps, however, Schweitzer realized all this. Perhaps he chose this period of history because he saw within it broad, undulating forces at work which do not present themselves so clearly to the view of the historians and social philosophers whose task it is to record and study surface events and subsurface trends. Perhaps the forces in the world-view of which Schweitzer spoke lie deeper and its swells move in slower rises and falls. Perhaps, as Schweitzer said, humanity's whole journey through history has been its search to understand the world and itself in order to form an adequate outlook upon life in which the deepest needs and cravings of its soul may be brought into a working harmony with what it knows about the world, a world-view which shall orientate the noblest aspirations of the heart with the grim facts of existence, so that the tendencies and potentialities within humanity may be fully realized in the best way possible. The eighteenth century, according to Schweitzer, found a world-view which carries within it such ingredients necessary for the success of all civilizations. Other ages, such as that, for example, in which the Stoics lived, also possessed these elements. Some ages possessed them to a greater, some to a lesser degree. Schweitzer felt that the Enlightenment did have and did utilize them to a greater degree.

Therefore, regardless of whether some of the philosophers of this period are antithetical to Schweitzer's own views, regardless of whether this age gave rise to forces which he found detrimental to our civilization, and despite the fact that the optimistic-ethical world-view faded and the scientific movements of the time discredited rational thought, natural law, religion, etc., despite even the fact that many of the reforms and accomplishments of the eighteenth century were later undone, still it is the enthusiastic and progressive spirit of the age, which looked forward to and labored for the time "when reason, having attained a position of permanent sovereignty, will put every human being in possession of the rights which belong to humans as humans, and will establish purposive and ethical relations in every department of life,"[18] that Schweitzer championed. When these reasons are kept in mind, perhaps his high evaluation of the age will not seem as erroneous as before.

When he referred to basing our world-view on "rational thought," he is making a plea that we bring into play all our deepest resources of reason. If Schweitzer used the word "rationalism," which he did, how is it distinguished from the word "rational," if at all?

Schweitzer realized that the reaction of the Romantic movement and the twentieth century against Rationalism is partly justified, for the "intellectual properties of the periods which we designate historically as the rationalistic are incomplete and unsatisfactory."[19] But he is adamant that "rational thought is more than a movement in history, it is a necessary phenomenon in all normal spiritual life."[20] The mine shaft which Rationalism sunk into the ground produced "only metal of small value," but this does not mean that it was digging in the wrong place, it just did not go down far enough to the rich strata which lay beneath its claim. Humanity has lost its confidence in the efficacy of reason to solve its problems. But this was the belief of the *Aufklarung* which made it great; a belief which we have abandoned. Even though Schweitzer realized that during the eighteenth century speculative thought soared to fantastic and unrealistic heights and that it often distorted reality, the basic principle which it utilized contained within it elements which are vital to any philosophy which desires to occupy itself with the elemental problems of life. Philosophy today looks with "condescending pity on the rationalism which she had outstripped. She prided herself on having got beyond the ideas of Kant . . . and on being at work today in close sympathy with the natural sciences."[21] But for this she is "poorer than the poorest rationalism."[22]

One wonders why, since the Enlightenment period "chose the right place for its digging," and since it possessed the proper world outlook, it did not strike the right vein of success? Schweitzer answered simply that it did not possess the adequate tools and the large storehouse of facts which scientific advancements brought to light. (While on one hand he criticized our age for its scientism, on the other hand he recognized science as an essential element, not only for human advancement in general, but for the particular type of rationalism which he advocates.) He wrote, "Philosophical, historical and scientific questions with which it was not capable of dealing overwhelmed the earlier rationalism like an avalanche, and buried it in the middle of its journey."[23] Because of this, the succeeding age lost confidence in its methods and left it buried. Schweitzer made a plea for a new rationalism and methodology.

> The new rational world-view must work its way out of this chaos. *Leaving itself freely open to the whole influence of the world of fact,* it must explore every path offered by reflection and knowledge in its effort to reach the ultimate meaning of being and life, and to see whether it can solve some of the riddles which they present.[24]

Notes

[1] Albert Schweitzer, "The Goethe Prize Address," *Goethe. Four Studies*, ed. by Charles R. Joy (Boston: The Beacon Press, 1949), p. 168.

[2] *Ibid.*, p. 179.

[3] *Ibid.*, p. 167.

[4] *Ibid.*, p. 169.

[5] *Ibid.*

[6] *Ibid.*, p. 172.

[7] *Ibid.*, p. 173.

[8] *Ibid.*, p. 172.

[9] *Ibid.*, p. 171, 172.

[10] *Ibid.*, p. 172, 173.

[11] George Seaver, *Albert Schweitzer: The Man and His Mind* (New York: Harper & Brothers, 1947), p. 336.

[12] Albert Schweitzer, *Philosophy of Civilization* (New York: The Macmillan Co., 1949), p. 148.

[13] Seaver, *Albert Schweitzer,* p. 336.

[14] Schweitzer, *Philosophy of Civilization*, p. 175.

[15] Magnus C. Ratter, *Albert Schweitzer: Life and Message* (Boston: The Beacon Press, 1950), p. 156.

[16] Ernst Cassierer, "Albert Schweitzer as Critic of Nineteenth Century Ethics," *Albert Schweitzer Jubilee Book*, ed. by A. A. Roback (Cambridge: Sci-Art Publishers, 1945), p. 248 ff.

[17] Pitirim A. Sorokin, *Social Philosophies of an Age of Crisis* (Boston: The Beacon Press, 1950), p. 269.

[18] Schweitzer, *Philosophy of Civilization*, p. 179.

[19]John Wild (ed.), *Spinoza: Selections* (New York: Charles Scribner's Sons, 1930), p. 54.

[20]*Ibid.*

[21]*Ibid.*

[22]*Ibid.*

[23]*Ibid.*, p. 55.

[24]*Ibid.* (italics mine).

CHAPTER NINE

The Delicate Balance:
The Preacher and the Scholar
From notes by Jackson Lee Ice; compiled by M. Marie Ice
1992

The problem which faced Schweitzer as a young scholar and a practicing Christian minister, faces many ministers—being faithful to one's religious beliefs and faithful to the truth of historical and scientific facts. Many leave the ministry because they cannot reconcile the two. Others wear two hats in an uneasy bifurcation of existence refusing to sacrifice the fruits of either, grasping paradox to their bosom as their saviour.

Not until the publication of his sermons was it known how important a part of Schweitzer's life his preaching was. Most overlooked this dimension of his life. If considered at all, it was regarded as peripheral. But the recent appearance of two books containing together twenty-nine out of three hundred sermons preached by Schweitzer at St. Nicholas' Church in Strasbourg between 1900-1913 and 1918-1921, interestingly changed that. It was for many of us an occasion for reconsideration. As D. Elton Trueblood wrote, ". . . by the publication of some of his sermons, we have a revelation of certain sides of a remarkable life of which we were formerly unaware"[1] It seemed a reappraisal of some of his theological ideas was appropriate.

Over the years, many writers, myself included, have stressed the heretical strains in Schweitzer's thought characterizing him as "a radical," "an agnostic" and "a humanist." Such descriptions are a familiar part of Schweitzerian scholarship and are well documented, as illustrated by his self-designation, "I am an agnostic in the following of Christ," and by his inability to accept the Virgin Birth, the Bodily Resurrection or the Divinity of Jesus. But accurate as such facts are of him, they always seem to leave something out of account. I believe his sermons now attest to this. There is a wealth of biographical facts and sermonic writings, and a series of articles on the New Testament published under the title *Gesprache Uber Das Neve*

Test, which reflect his deep, personal attachment to the Christian faith. Although known, these were soft-peddled because it seemed his scholarly writings minimized their importance. Now, in the light of his sermons, such facts once again come to the fore, and after insinuating themselves into one's consciousness raise some intriguing questions regarding Schweitzer's theological beliefs. They help to fill out the portrait of this complex personality with subtler hues. I am suggesting for the sake of sheer balance it may do well for his Christian critics, as well as for us pick-lock analysts, to seriously reconsider his preaching—the fifth dimension—so it may be included in the compass of our objective understanding.

There was always a curious reticence on the part of Schweitzer to speak of his religious development. It is not known if he underwent any modifications of his earlier religious faith. We are not told, for instance, how as a student at the Universities of Strasbourg or Berlin his studies might have changed his mind, or how his research on the *Quest* influenced his faith, or how, if at all, he was ideologically affected by the primitive harshness of the African jungle and the destructive consequences of World War I. He felt strongly that no one had any right to pry into another's private life and thoughts. So we are left mainly in the shadows about the exact landscape of his spiritual pilgrimage.

True, a brief discussion of his involvement in the Christian ministry as a young student and of his theology as reflected in his sermons will not resolve the enigmas surrounding him and his religious slant. It will not finalize to everyone's satisfaction, for instance, the otiose issue as to whether Schweitzer was really a Christian or a closet humanist. Nor will it help locate him neatly on some theological map. But this is not the point. I contend it will aid in attaining a more accurate view of understanding and appreciation of his personal faith.

I

As preface to his sermons, a review of a few telling facts are in order.

1. It is obvious Schweitzer's early childhood was molded by his Christian upbringing. His father as well as his maternal grandfather were Lutheran ministers. He regularly attended his father's church, participated in family prayers and Bible readings, and was baptized and confirmed in the Lutheran faith. The spiritual inspiration and protection of the "Lord Jesus" surrounded his early life like the Vosges Mountains of Alsace, which he loved, and were as natural to him as the bilingual community in which he lived.

2. As a student at the University of Strasbourg he studied Bible and Theology, served as assistant minister at St. Nicholas', and occasionally

substituted for his father in Gunsbach. At twenty-five years of age he was ordained into the Lutheran ministry. At twenty-six he was called to be the full-time pastor of St. Nicholas'. Along with his many scholastic duties, he regularly conducted services, taught Sunday School and held confirmation classes. At that time, he also had a responsible post as the deputy Principal of St. Nicholas' Theological College. What he wrote about his confirmation classes, which met three times a week, is revealing:

> The aim of my teaching was to bring home to their hearts and thoughts the great truths of the Gospel, and to make them religious in such a way that in later life they might be able to resist the temptation to irreligion which would assail them. I tried also to awaken in them a love for the Church and a feeling of need for a solemn hour for their souls in the Sunday service.[2]

3.   After he received his doctorate in philosophy at twenty-four, he applied for a teaching fellowship. In order to receive it he had to decide which scholastic path to follow: philosophy or theology? He was advised by his professor that it would be expedient, if he planned to teach philosophy, to separate himself from theology and his ministerial duties. In the face of this advice, Schweitzer purposely chose the pastorate and theology. "To me," he said, "preaching was a necessity of my being."[3]

After he entered medical school and had to give up his teaching and preaching, he remarked, "[N]ot to preach anymore, not to lecture anymore, was for me a sacrifice, and until I left for Africa I avoided, as far as possible, going past either St. Nicholas' or the university, because the very sight of the places . . . was too painful for me."[4]

4.   His momentous decision to become a medical missionary was due to a simple calling in the spirit of Jesus to serve others in need. Apparently, no more or no less. Though it meant the relinquishing of all professional posts and the foregoing of all future opportunities for such scholastic fame, he was more than willing to follow his resolve. He saw nothing unusual about it; to him it was not some complex, heroic act. Indeed, he regarded it as a privilege that he had the means and stamina to pursue what he freely chose to do with his life. He was anguished that even his family and closest friends did not understand his decision which to him was the logical and natural result of taking the call of Jesus, "Follow thou me," seriously. When pressed why he chose this particular expression of Christian service, he said, "I went to Africa because the Lord Jesus commanded me to go."

5.   Since his childhood he exhibited a great sensitivity to the suffering of all sentient creatures. His empathetic nature, his strong sense that fortune obligates, and his moral concern for the plight of the disenfranchised were dominant features of his personality throughout his life. His ethical predilections appeared early on and led him to make startlingly mature decisions

even as a child. It is only natural, perhaps inevitable, that he would find his spiritual mentor in the loving care and active devotion of Jesus who was part of his existence from the very beginning. His being "taken a prisoner by Jesus," as he expressed it, was not due to an exaggerated sense of sin or a frenetic need of psychic healing, but simply to finding in the Man from Nazareth a kindred spirit of compassion whom he felt called to serve.

6. Every Sunday, at his jungle hospital in Lambaréné, he held multi-lingual services for the natives, which consisted of a Bible reading, a brief and simple sermon, a prayer and a singing of a hymn He also regularly observed the practice of reading the Bible, reciting the Lord's Prayer and the singing of a hymn with his staff at the end of the evening meal.

He said he explained Jesus to the natives in his sermons as "the King of our hearts, who was sent by God." And when "I describe Jesus as He who brings peace with God into the hearts of men and women—they understand Him .... Whatever I make my starting point, I always lead on to the innermost fact involved in becoming a Christian, namely the being led captive by Christ ... "⁵

7. On one occasion when he discovered one of his nurses had never formally been consecrated a Christian, he insisted on baptizing her privately. Also, when he learned that his four grandchildren, whom he had not yet seen, were still devoid of the blessings of the Church, he insisted that they all be baptized by him when he returned to Europe. And they were.

Apparently such rites were of greater religious importance to Schweitzer than most readers realized. One wonders just how important to him other traditional beliefs and rituals were. Whether his sermons help to answer this question or not, they give us, according to their editor, "a more immediate glimpse of [his] piety than do his published writings."⁶

II

The first book of Schweitzer's sermons, *Strassburger Predigten* was published under the English title *Reverence for Life* [Harper & Row, 1969] and contains 17 selections delivered on different occasions between 1900-1919. The second collection, *Was Sollen Wir Tun*, was published in English as *A Place for Revelation* [Macmillan, 1988] and contains 12 sermons preached between February and August of 1919.

The sermons are characteristically brief, based almost exclusively on New Testament texts, expressed in simple, non-doctrinal language and replete with homey illustrations. He said of himself that "he preached not as a theologian but as a layman" and often felt apologetic about it.

Several things strike the reader about the content of these sermons.

First, one is conscious of his pastoral concern for the spiritual needs of his congregation.   Many titles reflect this: "The Courage of Action"; "Gratitude: the Secret of Life"; "Creative Suffering"; "Fulfill Your Destiny"; "Overcoming Death"; "The Peace of God."

Here Schweitzer speaks on hope:

> And now, there is one word I want to emphasize in the saying of our Savior. That is the most mysterious word in the whole sentence: "All." I will draw all men unto me—all. We know how few allow themselves to be drawn to him and we must ask ourselves: Are we among those who allow themselves to be drawn to him? How many insist on going their own way, the way to ruin? And yet our Savior promises: I will draw *all* men to myself. What hope this word gives us! Hope that even those who appear lost will be saved by the power of the cross of Christ, although we cannot understand how. What comfort such a faith is for the heart of many a poor mother who is mourning over a misguided child—and for many others as well. A veil of mystery lies over many questions—but in hope and in faith we grasp the mystery.[7]

On Christian responsibility:

> The plowman does not pull the plow. He does not push it. He only directs it. That is just how events move in our lives. We can do nothing but guide them straight in the direction which leads to our Lord Jesus Christ, striving toward him in all we do . . . We must take life seriously. I regard that as an obligation we owe to Jesus. I want others to sense that . . . . I want them to see that every moment we are conscious of our responsibility to our Lord for what our existence means to the people around us and what it means for the coming of the Kingdom of God in the world.[8]

On eternal life:

> Perhaps one has talked too much and too superficially about immortality, in order to comfort people in the face of death. Hence the word has been depreciated. Immortality believed in for the sake of comfort is not genuine immortality . . . .
>
> But the man who dares to live his life with death before his eyes, the man who receives life back bit by bit and lives as though it did not belong to him by right but has been bestowed on him as a gift, the man who has such freedom and peace of mind that he has overcome death in his thoughts— such a man believes in eternal life because it is a present experience, and he already benefits from its peace and joy.[9]

Second, it is interesting to discover that the first public expression of his philosophy of Reverence for Life is found in his sermons. A series of three preached in 1919 appears in *A Place for Revelation*. We have in these sermons the first fruits of the ideas which had been germinating since his internment as a prisoner of war in 1914, and which eventually were published in his *Philosophy of Civilization*. Apparently he believed it was important to share his most profound ideas with his congregation. Schweitzer was suspicious of convoluted thought; to him the most profound ideas were also the simplest. In a way his congregation served as one of the parameters for assaying the significance and clarity of his thought. For those who wish to grasp some of the subtler aspects of his ethic, it is most helpful to have it stated also in sermonic form.

An interesting aside to this is Schweitzer's view of the function of philosophy in general. According to him one of the major causes for the decay of Western Civilization was "philosophy's renunciation of her duty"[10] For him "the value of any philosophy is in the last resort to be measured by its capacity, or incapacity, to transform itself into a living philosphy of the people."[11] But philosophy neglected to do this. "Her way lay apart from the general spiritual life . . . . Refusing to concern herself with elemental problems, she contained no elemental philosophy which could become a philosophy of the people."[12] His indictment is not against any particular school, but against the very character of philosophic thought itself; what matters is not so much the answers to certain questions but the questions themselves. And here philosophy has failed—it has forgotten that universal function that philosophy has to fulfill in humankind's social, political and cultural life.

Schweitzer's *Philosophy of Civilization*, which is mainly a working out of his world-view of Reverence for Life, was his attempt to remedy this. But first, through his sermons, he also attempted to fulfill the function of a philosopher—to bring directly to the people, in words they could understand, a philosophy of life which offered an ethical world-view that was meaningful and life-giving.

> . . . It is useless simply to rehearse and interpret the ethical commandments of Jesus again and again, as if that would somehow in the end produce their general acceptance . . . . We must first of all create a *foundation for understanding* those commandments and guide our world into a frame of mind in which Jesus' teachings have meaning.[13]
>
> . . . And thus the final result of knowledge is the same, in principle, as that which the commandment to love requires of us. Heart and reason agree together when we desire and dare to be persons who attempt to fathom the depths of things.
>
> And reason discovers the connecting link between love for God and love for man: love for all creatures, reverence for all being, a compassionate sharing of experience with all of life, no matter how externally dissimilar to our own.
>
> . . . That is the beginning and the foundation of all ethics.[14]

Schweitzer's thoughts are also at times fearlessly frank:

Nature is beautiful and sublime viewed from the outside. But to read in its book is horrible. And its cruelty is so senseless.[15]

The God of love who meets us in love cannot be united with the God who encounters us in nature. The ethical law cannot be made consonant with the laws of nature.[16]

Thus, for everyone who truly gets acquainted with life, there comes a crisis in which this existence becomes worthless to him, even though he still carries on with it. Only reverence for life can lead us out of that crisis: we live out our duty. There is a deeper sense in the idea that we must all be born again in order to be what God requires of us. We must all be born again from the unconscious will to live [survival] to the higher, conscious will [reverence] in which we then live. Because life in itself is so dark, it remains so inexplicable, it appears to us as puzzling precious. In the confused noise of the world, we hear the eternal song of life like a pure, clear melody suspended over the whole and allow ourselves by this means to manage whatever our fate may be.[17]

Last, one cannot help notice the deep, personal piety which suffuses all his sermons. As one editor put it, his "proximity and relationship with Jesus Christ glows through everything like a hidden fire."[18]

Schweitzer writes:

Let me explain it my way. The glorified body of Jesus is to be found in his sayings. For he said of these, "Heaven and earth will pass away, but my words will not pass away." And this is the bodily form in which his spirit is constantly incarnated within human spirit. This is how he offers himself to men in the Holy Communion.... That is the Real Presence, where a man in spiritual hunger and thirst has taken the word of Jesus into Himself in order to love. This word was intended for Him, for that is where the living Jesus bound himself to that word. His life passed into the life of man, creating peace and joy.[19]

This is why our human will must become one with the all-powerful will of Jesus. Then a communion with him will be created, and men will experience the meaning of his promise: "I am with you."[20]

Finally, be true to Jesus and His spirit, for Jesus' spirit is the secret of true life. It teaches us what life demands from us. We are His disciples, not because we are immune to human frailty but because we must serve Him. And we have to serve Him because He lives among us, because He spiritually cares for us and suffers for our times.

This faithfulness toward Jesus is not a sort of complicated, mystical notion that sounds quite impressive in sermons but has no meaning in practical life. Far from it. Whoever has looked into the eyes of Jesus as He appears to us in His words knows that true happiness consists of service to this great One and His Spirit.[21]

"A great deal of personal confession is revealed in these sermons. They show us the unity of theology, faith and life in this great man. What we encounter page after page, what raises us up, moves, helps, and sustains us, is the warmth of a deep Christian piety that lives in constant intimate contact with Christ."[22]

III

Schweitzer's piety then—the fifth dimension—is not some incongruent appendage, something attached nostalgically or expediently to his life. It is there as a motivating force at the beginning and underlies all his other dimensions. Regardless of the agnostic outcroppings of his incomplete philosophy of life, or the heretical conclusions that he inevitably drew from his research on the historical Jesus , we are forced to admit, in view of the added evidence of his sermons, that his roots ran deeper into Christian soil than we realized and that the ruling, spiritual center of his life was, from first to last, the "Lord Jesus."

Factual knowledge about the outer, physical world, or historical knowledge about Jesus, is one thing; knowing the Universal Will-to-Love and the spiritual risen Christ within, is another. And it is this latter kind of knowledge that has transforming power and was, for Schweitzer, the essence of the Christian message.

If his particular form of Christian allegiance is still puzzling, if it is too radical or too orthodox sounding, or just strangely inconsistent with his other writings, then perhaps an answer lies in the fact that like all Giants of the Spirit, Schweitzer created his own dimension and defied traditional categories. Perhaps in the last analysis it is not a matter of acceptance or rejection but only an occasion for silent wonder, a feeling of gratitude that he lived among us, and for us, and the realization that God's house surely contains many dimensions.

Notes

[1] Albert Schweitzer, *Reverence for Life*, trans. Reginald H. Fuller, ed. Ulrich Neuenschwander (New York: Harper & Row, 1969), Foreword, p. 7.

[2] Albert Schweitzer, *Out of My Life and Thought* (New York: Henry Holt, 1950), p. 27.

[3] *Ibid.*, p. 25.

[4] *Ibid.*, p. 111.

[5] George Seaver, *Albert Schweitzer: The Man and His Mind* (New York: Harper & Brothers, 1947), pp.121-2.

[6] *Reverence*, p. 152.

[7] *Ibid.*, p. 23.

[8] *Ibid.*, pp. 47-8.

[9] *Ibid.*, p. 75.

[10] Albert Schweitzer, *The Philosophy of Civilization* (New York: Macmillan, 1949), p. 3.

[11] *Ibid.*, p. 7.

[12] *Ibid.*, p. 6.

[13] Albert Schweitzer, *A Place for Revelation: Sermons on Reverence for Life,* trans. by David Larrimore Holland, ed. by Martin Strege and Lothar Stiehm (New York: Macmillan, 1988), p. 5.

[14] *Ibid.*, p. 11.

[15] *Ibid.*, p. 15.

[16] *Ibid.*, p. 22.

[17] *Ibid.*, pp. 35-6.

[18] *Reverence*, p. 152.

[19] *Ibid.*, pp. 65-6.

[20] *Ibid.*, p. 34.

[21] *Ibid.*, pp. 85-6.

[22] *Ibid.*, p. 153.

CHAPTER TEN

His Legacy of Hope
1961

Norman Cousins tells of a French professor who in 1957 asked his students in an examination: "How would you define the best hope for the culture of Western Europe?" He received as one of the replies: "It is not in any part of Europe. It is in a small African village and it can be identified with an eighty-two-year-old man."

This nineteen-year-old student is not alone in his opinion; even today, many find in Albert Schweitzer a significance which goes beyond the ordinary. Thousands of concerned individuals, reflecting upon the needs of our complex age, seem to realize that the image of Schweitzer is growing taller and casting a larger shadow. They agree with Ernest Toch who, dedicating his Second Symphony to Schweitzer, wrote: "To the man who kindled this work in me, the only victor in a world of victims, the only seer in a world of darkness." I believe Albert Einstein felt this when he remarked: "There in this sorry world of ours is a great man."

In trying to determine what is meant by calling Schweitzer "great," I do not think it is due to his amazing feat of earning four PhDs and some seven honorary degrees, nor is it due to the fact that he has had many honors conferred upon him, among them the Order of Merit from Great Britain and the Nobel Peace Prize; nor do I believe it is due to his scholarly contribution of some twenty outstanding books and numerous articles and essays; nor is his life of self-sacrifice and service to some of the underprivileged peoples in Africa the sole reason for his greatness. These are important and most impressive, to say the least. But I believe so many have found him "the only seer in a world of darkness" because of the message he brings of which he is a living embodiment—Reverence for Life. "It is not so much what he has done for others," writes Norman Cousins,

but what others have done because of him and the power of his example. This is the measure of the man. What has come out of his life and thought is the kind of inspiration that can animate a generation. He has supplied a working demonstration of reverence for life.

His ethical philosophy is capable of giving to modern humanity four essentials: an imperative for intellectual honesty, a motive for existence, a reason for courage and a guide for action.

Whatever else modern humankind requires of a world-view, it must be intellectually honest. We now know too much to be satisfied with anything but the truth. The ethical philosophy of Schweitzer demands sincerity and honesty in the sacred realm of thought, no less than in all areas of life. It lays an obligation on our shoulders in the form of an imperative that we revere truth enough to seek it, and bring it to light. If the moral life is once again to have any influence over our minds and become a powerful civilizing force amongst us, it must come to the realization of Schweitzer that "the beginning of all spiritual life of any value is courageous faith in truth and open confession of the same." This intimate connection between the ethical life and the search for truth is wisely noted by Bertrand Russell: "The impartiality which, in contemplation, is the unalloyed desire for truth is the very same quality of mind which in action is justice, and in emotion is that universal love which can be given to all."

Unfortunately in our times the two have been divorced from each other. This can be illustrated by the sad thought that religion reveres life, but not truth enough, and that science reveres truth, but not life enough. Where knowledge and spiritual thought have renounced each other, we have a declaration of spiritual bankruptcy.

With the appearance of the philosophy of Reverence for Life all areas of human endeavor are brought into fearless relation to knowledge and analytic thought. This is certainly true of religion.

According to Schweitzer no more can religion afford to be established upon any kind of supernaturalism or infallible dogma. It has too often maintained allegiance to a special passage of scripture or to a tradition at the expense of the Christian spirit itself. "The situation today," writes Schweitzer,

> is that religion has completely withdrawn into itself, and is concerned only with the propagation of its own ideas, as such. It no longer sees any use in proving them to be in agreement with thought, but prefers that they be regarded as something altogether outside, and occupying a superior position. It loses thereby its connection with the spiritual life of the times and the possibility of exercising any real influence upon it.

Such a fearless quest for truth may bring a "painful disenchantment," but at least we will know what we are about, and we can take heart in the belief that "every new truth means ultimately something acceptable to reason." This is why Schweitzer can say:

> I was convinced—and I am so still—that the fundamental principles of Christianity have to be proved true by reasoning, and by no other method: reason, I said to myself, is given us that we may bring everything within the range of its action, even the most exalted ideas of religion. And this certainly filled me with joy.

Science, no less than religion, must also face the fact that it has not been completely honest. This is seen in the fact that it has equated truth too narrowly with the numerical statistical method, whereby mathematical equations, instead of being regarded as predictable calculations supporting human descriptions, are equated with reality, and taken to be more real than reality itself. We have become mere spectators in the drama of existence, and the human element has been denied any part, except in a deterministic manner which dehumanizes it, in science's views of the universe. It is most interesting to note that several eminent scientists now believe that science is more genuinely scientific in spirit when it takes into account the reasons why it cannot be utterly objective in its methods and claims. They state that human beings as participators and not mere observers are an intimate and important factor in the knowing situation.

Schweitzer, with his usual incisiveness points out:

> Today thought gets no help from science, and the latter stands facing it independent and unconcerned. The newest scientific knowledge may be allied with an entirely unreflecting view of the universe. It maintains that it is concerned only with the establishment of isolated facts, since it is only by means of these that scientific knowledge can maintain its practical character; the coordination of the different branches of knowledge and the utilization of the results to form a world philosophy are, it says, not its business. Once every man of science was also a thinker who counted for something in the general spiritual life of his generation. Our age has discovered how to divorce knowledge from spiritual thought, with the result that we have, indeed, a science which is free, but hardly any science left which reflects.

Our world is in too dangerous a position to allow half-truths and falsehoods to continue to become current among us. We must all become ethical enough to see the necessity of permitting deep thought to ply its trade in every level of life. It can bring the wider perspectives which are the only possible correctives for the multiple provincialism, divisive intolerance and truncated views which are a major source of confusion and misery. Without the purging discipline of intellectual honesty, humanity will destroy itself in unbridled excess. Reverence for Life which means reverence for truth is the essential partner in our perennial pilgrimage.

Schweitzer's ethical philosophy also gives us a motive for existence. Perhaps the most profound aspect of Schweitzer's thought lies in his personal struggle to remain intellectually honest and at the same time to give meaning to human existence. It is his great contribution that he continues to vindicate a human nature which twentieth century thought, armed with the latest theories, keeps repudiating. In his ardent attempt to found his ethical world-view upon a solid ground, he has illuminated our basic dilemma in the realm of values: the gross inconsistency between what mankind wills and what in fact existence actually offers. It is his determined movement through the chilling absurdities and painful enigmas of existence, and his arrival at last at a momentous affirmation of humanity, that marks him as a pioneer in thought.

Schweitzer would be the first to agree that what our knowledge tells us about the world, wars against any optimism about ultimate purpose or a universal moral order. This is what we would like to find, but this way seems inevitably closed to us. The universe has no such meanings which we can discern. Our knowledge-facts of the outer maneuverings of nature only leave us more and more puzzled and less and less optimistic. Life is ultimately a mystery.

> We cannot understand what happens in the universe. What is glorious in it is united with what is full of horror. What is full of meaning is united to what is senseless. The spirit of the universe is at once creative and destructive— it creates while it destroys and destroys while it creates; it remains to us a riddle. Inevitably we must resign ourselves to this.

But we need not resign ourselves to the belief that the meaning of life must be bent down to fit the knowledge of the world. We are foolish to wait upon specialized studies to construct for us a single theory of the universe which meets the demands of the spiritual life. It may be true that we can discern no purpose in history, or in the world at large which satisfies thought, but this does not mean we are without wisdom as to how we are meant to live.

Our inner convictions which go beyond the items of knowledge gathered from the world find their source in the mysterious Life-Force of which we are all a part. Schweitzer is convinced that if thought is deep and sensitive enough it will arrive at this profound knowledge, which is knowledge of the will-to-live. Humankind already, by reason of its inner will-to-live, affirms life. Pessimism is hence inconsistent. There is within humans the transcending powers of thought, symbolic communication, memory, creative imagination, freedom, sensitivity to pain and suffering in others, and, above all, concern for life. Why this is so is beyond us, but *that* it is so, is a fact. Life would perhaps seem absurd, if in the midst of the dark there was not this one illuminating fact—that we are all a part of the Life-Force which affirms life, which seeks to develop itself in the fullest way possible, and which exhibits a moral concern for what takes place in the world. This Urge-to-Life seeks within us all those meaningful aspects of existence which make life not only tolerable but triumphant. Humankind finds the resources for the meaning of life within itself.

> The Life-Force [says Schweitzer] is not a flame which burns only when it has the fuel of events which is desires; it even gives a pure, clear light when it has to depend on itself for nourishment. It shows as an actively working will even when surrounding events involve it in certain suffering. In profound reverence for life it makes existence, which, according to our ordinary motions, is in nor way any longer worthy of life, precious, in that in such beings also it develops and experiences its freedom from the world.

Here is a motive for existence—a deepened world- and life-affirmation, based upon the will-to-live, resulting in reverence for life; a reverence which is capable of taking into its circle of interest and concern the whole of life. In the mystique of moral action there flashes through the infinite opacity of the world a vision of fraternity; in loving self-devotion to other life we realize our spiritual union with other wills-to-live and thus with the Universal Will-to-Live; "I live my life in God," says Schweitzer, "in the mysterious ethical-divine personality which I cannot discover in the world, but only experience in myself as a mysterious impulse."

The world-view of reverence for life may, for many, seem too meager and unfinished to serve as a reason for courage. To recognize one's destiny within so simple an outlook is most difficult. Certainly, we think, the universe has more to offer than this by way of assuring our faith!

But, according to Schweitzer, if we are honest, it does not. In the past there have been those who have gone on to erect huge edifices of speculative ideas when the facts no longer supported their desires, and willing overpowered thought. Schweitzer openly admits that his philosophy of life is incomplete, for he is intellectually honest and he does not permit the desire for a world-view as a completed system, which seems impossible, to take precedence above the quest for value. And for him the world-outlook of reverence for life is enough.

So for Schweitzer, and others of our time who have bravely faced the ambiguities of human knowledge and the enigmas of existence, we can, and must, make do with the sober thought that what we do *not* know is immense, but what little we *do* know is sufficient to offer us a rational basis and courage for living. "I can do no other," says Schweitzer, "than hold on to the fact that the life-force appears in me as will-to-live which aims at becoming one with other wills-to-live. This fact is the light which shines in the darkness for me."

This same attitude was expressed by Albert Camus, the late French author-playwright, who like Schweitzer was pessimistic of knowledge ever bringing any easy solutions for the absurd forlornness of man's exile in existence. He too saw the chasm "between the mind that desires and the world that disappoints," and knew that the human voyager had only the compass of his own mind and heart to rely upon. He too rejected the spurious abstractions of superficial supernaturalisms. Yet he could say: "In the middle of winter I at last discovered that there was in me an invincible summer."

Schweitzer does not stop here, but moves stubbornly on to discover in this "invincible summer" an invincible moral will that binds all life together in a meaningful unity which gives humanity not only a reason for courage, but a stable guide to action. Its spiritual life is as a tree planted by the rivers of water which never run dry.

The guide for action which the moral philosophy of Reverence for Life gives us is quite direct and simple; it is easy to state, it is most difficult to fulfill. ". . . Evil is what annihilates, hampers or hinders life. Goodness is the saving or helping of life, the enabling of whatever life I can influence to attain its highest development." Reverence for Life consists in limitless responsibility towards all that lives; for the person "who is truly ethical all life is sacred." Here in Schweitzer's thought we find the ethic of Jesus taken from its apologetic framework, and made cosmic in scope. It is made more compelling for rational thought, and it is enlarged beyond the confines of a purely human matrix to encompass *all* life as a subject of moral concern.

Since Schweitzer believes all life is mysteriously one, he does not remain inconsistent and blunt in his natural sympathies by stopping short of animal or plant life, for these too are part of the sacred Life-Force and must be revered. Nor does he allow self-realization and devotion to others to stand in an unnatural or forced relation to each other: "Being true to the will-to-live in myself, I am true to it in others; and my altruistic actions pass imperceptibly over into a proper fulfillment of myself."

Schweitzer's ethic, however, is an "inexorable creditor," once it has taken hold, it never releases its grip, it refuses to allow one to live his life for himself alone; and it constantly expands one's horizon of moral responsibility.

The ethic of Reverence for Life constrains all, in whatever walk of life they may find themselves, to busy themselves intimately with all the human and vital processes which are being played out around them and to give themselves as men to the man who needs human help and sympathy. It does not allow the scholar to live for his science alone, even if he is very useful to the community in so doing. It does not permit the artist to exist only for his art, even if he gives inspiration to many by its means. It refuses to let the businessman imagine that he fulfills all legitimate demands in the course of his business activities. It demands from all that they should sacrifice a portion of their own lives for others. . . . What every individual has to contribute remains his own secret. But we must all mutually share in the knowledge that our existence only attains its true value when we have experienced in ourselves the truth of the declaration: "He who loses his life shall find it."

One day while I was speaking to the late Willard Sperry, Dean of Harvard Divinity School, he made the prophetic comment to me that in his opinion the ethic of reverence for life is simple and at the same time profound enough to become in the future a great and moving force in the world. He went on to say that in an age in which *irreverence* for life has become the dominant attitude, Schweitzer's reaffirmation of life in the spirit of true humanitarianism seems something more than important; it is a light that shines in the darkness, and whether the darkness comprehends it or not, that light may determine its fate.

Perhaps the young French student, who found that the best hope for the future of Western culture "resides in a small African village," is right. But at least we know that Albert Schweitzer's philosophy of Reverence for Life gives us four things which are essential to our success: an imperative for intellectual honesty, a motive for existence, a reason for courage and a guide for action.

Appendix

The following are selected preliminary notes of Jackson Lee Ice for his essay on *Schweitzer and Bach*, the fifth chapter of this book. They have been compiled by David Miller and Marie Ice for inclusion in this volume. Readers may be interested to compare both similarities and differences in interpretation and emphasis between the notes of Jackson Ice and the finished essay, written by musician and Schweitzer music scholar, Michael Murray.

OUTLINE

Section I
- ❏ Impact of Bach upon Schweitzer
- ❏ Interesting similarities between the two
- ❏ Parallels

Section II
- ❏ Music was Bach's religion. Bach was a mystic (this aspect appealed most to Schweitzer).
- ❏ What does this mean? How can music be religious or mystical? What relation does music have to the Universe and to the life of the spirit? (It inculcates a sense of reverence.)

Section III
- ❏ Now we can better understand Schweitzer's adulation of Bach and his remark that music was Bach's religion (in the deepest Christian sense of the word), his confession of faith, and an act of love of God.
- ❏ Meaning in music

NOTES

I

- ❏ I have read Schweitzer's epoch-making volumes on J. S. Bach several times and each time I am impressed with the amount of erudition and scholarship such a study required. In the midst of a very active time in his life, the young Schweitzer wrote with a clarity and confidence so typical of him. ... The Bach book was as much a challenge for Schweitzer as the Jesus book—an individual stand against consensus (this appealed to Schweitzer). At that time, this was a radical interpretation of Bach's (the Master's) music. I concur with James Brabazon, "No one, before or since, has combined such extensive technical knowledge with such aesthetic insight, enthusiasm and power to express himself."

However, a recent re-reading brought home another insight concerning Schweitzer: the strong tie he had throughout his life with Bach and the interesting, underlying similarities the two men shared. (There are certain traits of character which seem characteristic of both Bach and Schweitzer—whether by accident, or consciously acquired, is beside the point.)

❑ As Schweitzer benefitted from admired traits in all whom he met since childhood, he adapted many of Bach's traits and habits:
  • Daily routine, hard work, yet took time for others;
  • Concentration;
  • Not withdrawn from domestic life;
  • Religious, but not doctrinaire; orthodox in some ways; mystical belief; feeling of oneness;
  • Relaxed way of organ-playing; preference for simpler organ stops.
There has been an unthinking adulation of both, but no intimate insight into their similar lives—this seems hidden from biographers.

❑ Parallels:
  • Schweitzer accurately describes *himself* in these words regarding Bach: "He is ... a rare personality that does not become, but always is." (Bach's music and musical life seem unscathed by ordinary affairs; he moves to his own inner music; seems to work and live in his own self-made world—in a different dimension.)
  • Both disliked working under the imposition of any group, institution or governing body. *Very independent personalities.*
  • Both were not interested much in *religion*, but were very *religious*; individualistic need of traditional, institutional intermediaries between themselves and God.
  • Both had a mystical frame of mind. (Schweitzer admired Bach because his music ultimately served his religious beliefs and outlooks).
  • Both gained their knowledge from practical experience, working and reflecting on their own.

II

❑ If anything characterizes Bach's music it is the words of Paul, *"in the world, but not of the world."*

What Bach said of music is true of all art: *"it is the servant of God to help his sorrowful creatures, to give him joy worthy of their destiny."*

Mysticism—the key to Bach's mystical soul. Bach—the well-tempered mystic.

There is an air of consecration about Bach's musical compositions, for he did not compose them for recognition; he did not ask the world to be acquainted with them. He seemed to compose many of his pieces because he had to: they did not serve the purpose of gaining money or fame, nor did he write them out of joy for himself in his creative leisure.

He also didn't seem aware of the greatness of his works. They are produced untainted by self-conscious expression.

Schweitzer believed Bach's artistic activity was rooted in his piety. He made his art his religion, and an expression of joy—ineffable praise of (some Transcendent Power) God. An end in itself. "All great art, even if called secular, is really religious from his point of view."

His music seems to come from another dimension, unbothered by ordinary levels of daily life—truly harmonies of the spheres.

He expresses poetic and pictorial thoughts through the tonal motifs of his music. He transports his visions and feelings through tonal motifs to the creative imagination of the hearer, and engulfs him in moving, profound emotions; dimensions of the soul. Elemental vitality—structural perfection.

It does not delineate natural psychic phenomena. It is difficult to domesticate it. It does acquiesce to our demands or feelings; it soars above us. It is we who participate in its dimensions, in its ineffable drama, if we wish. It seems to move in a different sphere, effortlessly, triumphantly, a self-unfolding of multiple novel variations as if more than a human hand engineered such brilliant architechtonics. It purges all lowly connotations.

An illustration of Hegel's "self-unfolding of the Idea through dialectic stages of thesis, antithesis and synthesis."

An incomprehensive necessity as it struggles to overcome its own opposite and return in final self-realization in its finale.

To those who don't, or can't, participate in the world that Bach's music creates and inhabits, it seems cold, mechanical, tedious. Without the religious spirit, it is drained of its power.

❑ Religious Dimensions of Music

The intimate relation of music to religion and the religious experience (spiritual life) is not accidental.

Music is capable of opening up dimensions in the world and in ourselves, more poignantly and directly, as no other art can.

Listening to music is aesthetic because it thrusts us out of clock time into the presence of all time (temporality). It uses tempi to escape time.

Non-program music—or music designating religious, mystical emotions and ideas—is in no way *in time*. In program music we reflect about process (time and space); in abstract music we *directly encounter* process (for it avoids designative meaning to specific objects and events).

Music makes us ecstatic, makes us stand out from the self-conscious—we give ourselves up to music. We are open (to Being) (Oceanic feeling) and great music reveals something regarding the mystery. We *participate*—consciousness of unrealized possibilities necessary for such participative experience.

Bach is an exceptional example of inexhaustibility. His music possesses, at the same time, both designated and embodied meaning. It is a revelation of mystery.

All works of art are religious insofar as they reveal something of the mystery of Being, and pose the Existential.

Goethe: "I expressed it to myself as if the eternal harmony were communing with itself, as might have happened in God's bosom shortly before the creation of the world . . . . I seemed neither to possess nor need ears, still less eyes, or any other sense. You feel yourself at the center of the world."

III

❑ Bach's musical genius has done more to tender the Christian religion than most theologians verify. It is the felt presence of the Christian drama, of God's spirit and the living passion of Christ that enhances and enlivens the faith in the reality of the Christian vision more than all the creeds. For more and more church-goers, it is the meditative movement of the music where one meets—if at all—the living presence of the Holy, the Other, Depth Dimension of the quiet assurance of the Invisible Hand. A momentary glimpse of something so poignantly real and yet so illusive. A momentary stay against Chaos. How is music able to do this?

Bach's music moves in an atmosphere of his own—undisturbed and unbothered by other musical forms, by the pace of life and the march of time. It possesses its own time, its own space, an unearthly confidence and peace, a vision of the ultimate all its own—that draws us into its own dimension.

When the last days (trumpet) shall come, it will be the sound of Bach, not the jangled voices of theology that shall be our last joyous sustaining memory of the Christian dream. Of that which could in any way guarantee to the heart the endurance of the dream. Last (sustaining) support of faith, no noisy creedal guarantees for me . . . .

Music is an essential part of the Christian religious service, particularly the Protestant. But I wonder if many realize how essential?

Fundamental reality is made up of resonances mathematically (grasped) for calculation, and emotionally for the meaning of life.

Bach the mystic? Yes, for *mysticism is imaginative faith in tension with reality.*

❑ That music is incapable of conveying specific meaning apart from musical meanings seems specious to me. Anyone observing the multiple sounds that take place in nature as specific means of communication knows that such sounds are more than emotional out-pourings of sheer exuberance . . . . A certain timbre, tone, pitch and rhythm all have a particular meaning to the keen ears of a dog. Why not the subtle, multiform of musical sound found in a piece of music performing a similar function—not just emotional meanings, but sounds that possess cognitive meaning also for humans? Learn the motifs and some music can be a second form of speech— (metaphors straining toward specificity?).

Beethoven knew J. S. Bach as a young student, through his teacher, and studied his *Well Tempered Clavichord*, which he said was his musical Bible. He once remarked, *"Nicht Bach. Meer sollte er heissen!* ("Not a brook. He should be called a sea!")

Bach's music is how the mind sounds: the workings of the human mind verified and materialized for us in living sound. It stimulates the orderly (logical) part of our brains as well as the imagistic, intuitive parts, and unifies them. Both sides (left/right) of the brain.

Schweitzer admired Bach's dedication; love of Bible and music; "in the world, but not of the world"; sensitivity to religious emotions in his interpretation of *chorals*. His work and music were dedicated to God/Jesus.

Bach fashioned his music to the text.

Schweitzer played Bach "with a spiritual vision." . . . "What matters above all is the *spirit* in which Bach is presented. With each performance one should give something to the hearer; one should communicate the message of the music and set the hearer free from the realm of the mundane. The sounds should speak to him of peace and serenity, and of that gentleness from which we draw the power to keep on living. If Bach's music leads to this unique state of rapture, if in performances one can communicate something of it to others, then one has truly understood the master and may be called his true prophet (messenger; herald—*Verkünder*). We must not forget—and with this I shall close—that Bach is not only one of the greatest musicians; he is also one of the greatest mystics the world has ever produced."

Jackson Lee Ice

Jackson Lee Ice received his PhD from Harvard University in 1955 and began teaching at Florida State University that same year. His books include *Albert Schweitzer: Prophet of Radical Theology* and *The Death of God Debate*. He was a member of the Board of Directors of The Albert Schweitzer Fellowship and a former president of The Society for Philosophy of Religion. He died in 1991.

The Albert Schweitzer Institute for the Humanities

The Albert Schweitzer Institute for the Humanities—co-publisher of this volume—is dedicated to advancing the philosophy, ideals and humanitarianism of Dr. Albert Schweitzer (1875-1965). In the past year, ASIH has airlifted millions of dollars of medicine, medical equipment, clothing, school supplies and toys to victims of the ethnic war in the former Republic of Yugoslavia; hosted an international environmental symposium at the United Nations; presented its first annual Albert Schweitzer Environmental Youth Award; initiated an ongoing food and clothing drive at the local level that has already benefitted the homeless at more than half a dozen Connecticut shelters; begun preparations—in conjunction with Yale University School of Medicine—for a major medical conference to be held in August 1994; and launched the International Albert Schweitzer Lecture Series, also at Yale. In addition, the Institute is actively engaged in evacuating critically ill children from the former Yugoslavia and arranging for their medical treatment and care in U.S. hospitals.

A non-profit, non-governmental organization affiliated with the United Nations, The Albert Schweitzer Institute devotes itself to humanitarian action, research, education, and publication in the areas of Dr. Schweitzer's own endeavors: Health Care and Medical Relief, Disarmament and Demilitarization, Human Rights, Theology and Ethics, Environmental and Animal Issues, and Music and Arts.

The Institute is an evolution of the Albert Schweitzer Memorial Foundation, established in 1984 by Harold Robles with the support of Dr. Schweitzer's daughter, Rhena Schweitzer Miller. Since April 1993, ASIH has been affiliated with Quinnipiac College in Hamden, Connecticut.

For more information please write to: The Albert Schweitzer Institute for the Humanities, 515 Sherman Avenue, Hamden, Connecticut 06514. Telephone: 203-281-8926. FAX: 203-281-8929.